MotherHoot

For Mary Jo Porter —

Enjoy!

Margaret G. Bigger

MotherHoot

The Lighter Side of Motherhood

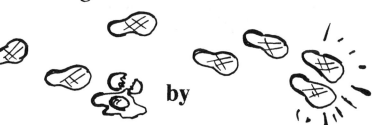

by

Margaret G. Bigger

Author of *There's No Such Thing as a Perfect Wedding*
and
You've GOT to Have a Sense of Humor to Have a Wedding

Illustrated by Loyd Dillon

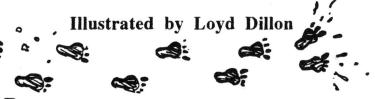

ABB   A. Borough Books

Copyright 1999 by Margaret G. Bigger

ISBN   0-9640606-8-X

Library of Congress Catalog Card Number: 98-71924

Printed in the United States of America

Cover design by Loyd Dillon
Illustrations by Loyd Dillon

ABB

A. Borough Books
P.O. Box 15391
Charlotte NC 28211

CONTENTS

Acknowledgements

So many people contributed personal stories to this book that I cannot possibly name them all. But I am deeply grateful to each one. You know who you are.

A few mothers either experienced more trials and traumas —or figured out how to laugh about them—or didn't suppress their memories. To these, I offer my special appreciation: Nan Millette - Houston, Texas, A. Fran Booth - Atlanta, Georgia, Sue Elrod, Robbye Dunning, Harriet Orth, Bert Barrett, Allison Elrod and Ethel Mc Millan - Charlotte, North Carolina, Maria Weed - Lincolnton, North Carolina and Bet Ancrum - Lake Wylie, South Carolina.

Thanks also to the parenting magazines that sponsored Funny Motherhood Stories contests or ran articles requesting stories for *MotherHoot*: *Our Kids 'N Teens* - Charlotte, North Carolina, *Parents Express* - Philadelphia, Pennsylvania, *Valleykids Parent News* - Batavia, Illinois, *Our Kids Atlanta* - Atlanta, Georgia, *Our Kids Houston* - Houston, Texas, *New Jersey Family* - Trenton, New Jersey, *Parents & Kids* - Jackson, Mississippi, *Carolina Parent* - Durham, North Carolina, *Parenting* (Herald-Journal) - Spartanburg, South Carolina, *Parents' Paper, ink* - Florence, South Carolina and *Wonderful!* - Midlands, South Carolina,.

And I am grateful to the radio talk show hosts who opened their mikes to me and encouraged listeners to call in their stories:

Valerie Simpson - WRVA, Richmond, VA
Dennis Sutton, Andy Rent - WCUZ, Grand Rapids, MI
Jeff Collins - WCCF, Punta Gorda, FL
Cameron Garrison - WBT, Charlotte, NC
John Wrisley - WSCQ, Columbia, SC
Greg Marshall - KLPW, Washington, MO
Mark Heimburger - WDWS, Champaign, IL
Carolyn Schultz - KQWC, Webster City, IA
Jordan Rich - WBZ, Boston, MA
Mark Stevens - WEW, St. Louis, MO
Janet Rose - WGOL, Lynchburg, VA
Jonathan and Diana Monk - KFSO, Fresno, CA
Shark Man - WLKG, Lake Geneva,WI
John Lanigan, John Webster, Jimmy Malone -
WMJI, Cleveland, OH

INTRODUCTION

Whatever the age of the kids, motherhood can be exhilarating or exasperating, sometimes both at the same time, but often exasperation exceeds exhilaration.

Think of it: we spend years preparing for our occupation outside the home, but most high schools and colleges never teach parenthood preparation! It's trial and error, mostly error.

This is a lifetime career which doesn't end with their graduation or marriage or our own retirement. It goes on and on and on and...

The best parents, experts say, have a sense of humor. Of course! When the frustration gets too great, you just have to laugh it off. Try it! You simply cannot giggle and scream at the same time.

Here's a collection of true stories about motherhood—most were told to me by mothers who can now chuckle about incidents which may not have seemed the least bit humorous at the time.

It's a celebration of the uniqueness and resiliency of mothers everywhere.

EXPECTANT, EXPECTORANT BEHAVIOR

There's a certain trauma to being pregnant, especially the first time. Morning sickness isn't always confined to morning. Little stresses become big ones. New daddies don't always understand, but siblings *think* they do.

Marian's friend Clarissa called to announce, "I don't know how it happened, but I'm pregnant!"

Ever after, whenever any of their mutual friends had anything momentous to report to one another, they began with "I don't know how it happened, but..."

They also wondered if Clarissa ever did figure out how it happened. She went on to have what Marian considered "an inordinate number of offspring."

Heidi's husband admitted to co-workers that he had a "thing" about her water breaking. Her baby was due in April, and in March he had already placed plastic on the rugs and sofa. He kept towels in the car for the uncertain emergency.

In early April, Heidi was talking with her mother on the phone, "Oh no!" she said in a near shout. "My water broke!"

Hubby rushed in with every towel from the bathroom.

She dropped the phone. "April Fool!"

In telling about the merciless trick she had played on him that morning, he simply couldn't understand why his colleagues were snickering.

Having frequented a particular Chinese restaurant for quite a while, Peggy nodded at the familiar hostess.

The Chinese lady smiled at Peggy's protruding stomach. "I know what you're going to have," she said knowingly. "A boy, because you're getting uglier."

"I was so pregnant," said Lettie Mae from Virginia, "I couldn't see that I'd worn mismatched shoes to work."

9

An older daughter of Italian immigrants in Michigan, Gabriella was the first in her family of 15 to visit a gynecologist.

"Next time you come in," he said, "bring in your urine." She looked at him rather curiously and left.

Two weeks later, she carried in two grocery bags filled with Mason jars.

During the '60s, gynecologists would allow pregnant women to bring in their specimens. As Sarah was preparing for a prenatal appointment, the only empty container she could find was a whiskey bottle. En route, she stopped at a drug store, leaving the specimen on the front seat of her car. While she was inside, the bottle was stolen.

Very pregnant, Florence, who is from Illinois, was tutoring at a city college in a micro-computer lab, when a secretarial class came into the lab. One young girl became super-agitated over her inability to use the printer and blamed the equipment.

The more Florence explained how to eject a sheet of paper, the more the student insisted that it was a faulty printer. Then as Florence was reaching over the printer to retrieve the paper, the baby kicked the printer offline and ejected two sheets of paper. "If the baby can do it, you can," Florence said.

Funny, the girl never held the printer accountable again.

While lunching in the food court, I could hear the kid's screams from one end of the mall to the other as the mother, more red-faced than the child, strolled and stopped, strolled and stopped, trying to calm him.

I hurried to finish so I could get to the nearby drug store. The tantrum howls followed. A pregnant woman beside me spoke to no one in particular over the din. "Someone remind me why I'm having this child."

"When I told my mother I lost my plug,*" says Tuppins, "she said they didn't have those in the '60s."

* For those pregnant during the '60s or before: she is referring to the mucus plug you lose right before the water breaks.

Those crazy cravings!

Leaving her daughter's play school, Janet had a few blessed hours to herself. She raced to satisfy her daily morning craving. "Peanut," her baby due, demanded M&Ms!

Entering a store, she pressed her car remote only to hear a familiar "chirp." Locked out! She grabbed some M&Ms but couldn't find 12-volt batteries. Distracted, she left empty-handed.

Neither the nearby drug store, jewelry shop or grocery had the right size batteries, but she found and purchased more marvelous M&Ms. Meanwhile, she was melting from the summer heat. An elderly stranger named Charlie offered to drive to an electronics store to get her some batteries. While waiting, Janet reached into her pocket for M&Ms. Alas, chocolate mush!

Aha! A vending machine. She dropped the coins in and selected you-guessed-it. Ugh! Cheese crackers plunked into the tray. Charlie returned with the batteries only to catch her tearfully lamenting her bad luck. She thanked him, unlocked her car and headed back to the play school.

Who should drive up at the school but Charlie with a fresh pack of M&Ms. "*You* needed recharging," he said.

Donna had an odd craving. The aroma of a hardware store stimulated her senses to heavenly heights. "Not just any hardware store would do," she said. "Only a certain one in the town we lived in at the time." She grinned. "I did whiff out others. They all disappointed me."

Well into her last trimester, she admitted her quirky craving to her brother. "I like to go into a hardware store and smell."

With typical brotherly concern, he mused, "Well, do they ask you to leave the store when the other customers become offended?"

You think YOU were stressed!

So what was a six-month pregnant woman from Ft. Smith, Arkansas, doing in an outback Australian inlet in the dark anyway? Kathy's hubby, a salesman for a fishing line company, wanted her to accompany him on a business trip. The Barra Classic, a fishing tournament, was held two hours outside of Darwin down a dirt road. The Classic was a daytime event, but he thought she would like to see a man catch a crocodile with his

bare hands. They joined cameramen in two flat-bottom boats one night to film this feat.

A line of crocodiles stood ashore until the men began spotlighting. Those big eyes shone as *whish, whoosh,* they slid into the water. As planned, a ranger pulled one out of the inlet and tagged him with his bare hands. The camera crew got cute and threw someone's hat into the water with an "Uh oh!"

Meanwhile the only one sitting down in either boat was the pregnant passenger, Kathy. Suddenly, a crocodile hit their boat. Water swirled over the bow. The guide shut off the engine. Another mammoth reptile knocked their craft, which flipped downward, filled with water, then flopped upside down. Stunned, Kathy sank beneath the surface, but remembering to follow the bubbles, she ascended to gasp for air. The others threw her atop the overturned hull.

A Catholic, Kathy started a "Hail Mary" and a prayer or two in disoriented desperation. "Oh, You know what I mean," she shrieked. "If You save us, I'll go to church."

"Shut up!" growled a fellow-drownee, afraid her voice would attract more trouble.

For a moment, all was quiet. Kathy thought she and her baby were safe. Not so!

They must get to shore fast by swimming. As they thrashed around, Kathy recalled reading how the aborigines always put their women, who were expendable, on the end of a line when crocodiles were threatening. "I'm getting in the middle!" she shouted and splashed her way to the center. The five others, all male, apparently hadn't read the same book. So they swam around her until they reached the shore. Safe at last!

Not quite. Deadly snakes were draped from the trees, lurching to strike. Kathy, her husband, the cameramen and guide trudged through the menacing thicket. Then they rejoiced to have gotten out unhurt. The sextet were still hugging each other when they realized that the mud to their knees was a buffalo wallow. Mean dogs were stalking around, seeking prey.

Just then, they heard the other boat coming to rescue them. One fearless photographer braved the thicket one more time to alert the others of their whereabouts. Guess what! They all had to retrace their steps!

Kathy was a wreck. Husband Bob never got his hair wet. But both were unnerved when the rangers expressed elation that they—and her baby—were all alive. "It was a miracle no one was eaten!" they kept saying. "It's mating season. The crocodiles are extra hungry."

Some men just don't "get it."

Nan overheard her husband talking on the phone one night. "Well, sure I could," he said. "My wife is expecting twins early in the new year, but once she has them, we would be ready to move. England sounds wonderful!"

Why do we lose self-esteem when we're pregnant? Comments like this from Tuppins may give a clue: "My husband says I look like a VW bug when I lie on my back."

Self-conscious about the squared-off shape of her feet, Janet from Lynchburg, Virginia, wore socks in the delivery room. "I wouldn't take them off," she recalled. "But everything else was out for the world to see."

Hubby, who often teased her about her ugly extremities was suddenly saying, "I was just kidding. I *love* your feet."

Hours later, he saw his daughter appear and exclaimed, "She's beautiful! She has my feet!"

Two weeks before her due date, the prospective mother was helping out at the office after hours. The company Lisa worked for was moving. At about 10:30 p.m., her water broke.

Male co-workers shook their heads. "We don't deliver babies," one said. "We just move furniture."

A quick call later, Lisa hurried to leave. Even with wet pants, she was giving goodbye hugs. One man came up real close. She reached to hug him, too.

"I don't want one," he said. "I just want the key to the computer."

While on vacation in Connecticut, Dottie and Fred stopped for lunch at a fine restaurant. When Dottie headed for the ladies room, Fred got up to pay the bill. After taking only a few steps, Dottie blacked out. The maitre d' and a waiter rushed to pick her up. Her husband helped the others drag her outside for air.

Bad plan. At the entrance, she got sick, a poor advertisement for restaurant business. Management personnel were profuse with apologies, refunded Fred's money and insisted on "doing something" for Dottie's comfort, bowing and scraping all the while. Dottie settled for tea and crackers in the bar. At last, she felt well enough to walk, and they got up to leave.

That's when Fred made the unforgivable statement of a lifetime. "It's okay," he told the manager. "She's pregnant. She does this all the time."

"It's time!" gasped the mom-in-labor from a gurney.

Dad jumped up, slipped down, conked his head and split it open. He got to the operating room before she did.

Oops!

"Nancy, are you pregnant?" Betty asked her daughter via an overseas phone call. (Let's not waste words.)

"No, Mother," said Nancy, a commander's wife at a U.S. Air Force base in Spain in the late '80s. "But just about every woman on the base is. You've never seen so many 18-year-olds in maternity uniforms."

"How do they do their jobs?" Betty wondered aloud.

"You should be asking, how could this happen?" Nancy said. "The dispensary handed out birth control pills that were out-of-date. The base had to call in three new obstetricians."

Count your blessings!

Every mother has a personal pregnancy story, but this Charlotte, North Carolina woman's is unique. Marguerite, you see, was told that she couldn't get pregnant. Some fertility treatments later, she conceived twins. Steven changed jobs so that they could move back to her hometown before the twins were born.

Motherhood seemed to agree with Marguerite, so when she found some leftover fertility medication, it was her idea to try again—but not for twins. The doctor would monitor carefully, so that if she were releasing multiple eggs, they'd call it quits.

Shazam! Too late after the first try. No twins, though. Triplets! Born when Megan and Matthew were two months into the terrible twos! Two plus three equaled 50 diaper-changes per day. Caroline, Ellie and Andrew had to nurse every four hours and still needed a formula supplement.

"Somehow," chuckled Marguerite, "I've become the Mother Teresa of mothers."

THE moment - natural and adoptive.

The pain in Trina's husband's belly was intense. She was in labor, but *he* was hurting. She had leaned forward to push and bit a bruise into his belly.

En route to the hospital, Mom said to Dad, the driver, "Honey, I think this baby is coming right now!"

He pulled to the shoulder of the highway to find out what he could do to help.

"Nothing! Drive!" she gasped.

And so he did.

Meanwhile, she put her feet on the dashboard and, in a few moments, caught her baby in mid-air.

Such a remarkable birth deserved a remarkable name: the location of his birth, Accord.

Time was when Dad was not allowed in the birthing room. No more. When Shelly had her baby, she was joined by her husband, her mother, her father and his new wife, her brother and his girl friend. They had to wake up little brother so he could see every drop of blood and afterbirth.

Adoptions are notorious for red tape, but because this baby was in a military hospital, the paperwork, protocol and procedures were horrendous. The prospective parents had jumped through all the hoops except checking out of the hospital. A friendly staff member as well as agency personnel had warned them that everything must be in perfect order when they stopped by the three windows before exiting. The mother held the inches-thick file, while the father presented the stack of carefully filled out forms at the first window.

"I don't know what this is all about," said the hospital employee. "Move on to the next window."

The next person said, "You have to check out over there."

At the third window, the father explained that they had everything in order.

"That'll be $18.37," said the clerk.

"What's that?" he asked beginning to simmer. "How'd you..."

Mother Allison's kick stopped him mid-sentence.

16

"Here's a twenty. Keep the change," he said, and they rushed out with their baby.

No one ever even glanced at their papers.

Children's interpretations:

Janet heard all about her own pregnancy from her 4-year-old daughter's preschool teacher.

Little Samantha had told the class that her mama was like a kangaroo, because she had a pouch, too. "Soon the doctor will unzip her tummy and get the baby out, but...(pause for thought) now Mom can't, you know, skip or jump or hop, 'cause it makes her throw up."

A Brandon, Mississippi mom called 5-year-old Brittany in to tell her about her soon-to-be baby sister. Stretched out on her bed, Janie asked, "Have you noticed that my tummy has been getting bigger?"

With encouragement, Brittany was rubbing the enlarged belly when the baby kicked, startling her.

"What do you think that was?" Janie asked.

Brittany brightened. "Jumping beans!"

Benny, 3, complained to Tonie of a boo-boo on his finger.

She asked him how he hurt it.

He said he had banged it long ago..."when I was born."

Tonie frowned.

"I hurt it on the abillical cord, because it had a sharp edge."

When Donna took Caitlin to visit a family member and her newborn in a Jackson, Mississippi hospital, the child observed that the patient had on a hospital gown, ID bracelet and an IV. She watched fascinated as the nurse wheeled in a bassinet and placed the newborn in her mother's arms.

Several months later, Caitlin was hospitalized for dehydration. This time, *she* was the one in the hospital gown and ID. Soon, a nurse came in and inserted an intravenous needle into her hand. When the nurse left, Caitlin looked over at Donna. "Is she going to get my baby, Momma?"

Beth from Wayne, Pennsylvania, was taking her daughters to a friend's house to see her newborn twins, a male and a female. She overheard their conversation in the back seat.

"When babies are born, how do you tell if it's a boy or a girl?" Kristen, the 6-year-old, wondered.

Colleen, 4, replied matter-of-factly, "Kristen, you know girls come out wearing pink and the boys are wearing blue."

Selena was trying to prepare her 2-year-old for the trauma of having a baby sister. She called him to her and said gently, "There's a baby in my tummy, and she's a girl."

"I know," he said, staring at her stomach, "and her name is Jamie."

Mom sucked in her breath. "Do you see anybody else in there?"

Stephen was staring at his mother, Debbie, who was eight months pregnant. She could tell that something was bothering him, as he came back and forth for second looks. "What's wrong?" she asked.

He was still staring. "Mommy, how did you eat that baby into your belly?"

In her eighth month of pregnancy, Lynn was still teaching in a North Carolina junior high school when she fractured a bone in her foot. There was no harm to the baby, but she had to miss a day of school.

On her return, one of her male students stared at her and her crutches and finally blurted out, "You mean you already had your baby?"

Mom was truly round and firm and fully-packed just before her daughter was born.

She understood her son's reaction, however, when she told him that he had a little sister.

"Oh," Timmy said forlornly. "I wanted a basketball."

WHO? WHY?

Undoubtedly, the first official act of parenthood is naming the child. Most mothers, and occasionally fathers, give this a great deal of thought. Some, however, don't look ahead far enough into the future.

A grandmother rushed up to me as I was entering the church where I worked. "Did you hear what we named the baby?"

I thought she had said "Sharmen" until she added, "you know, like 'please don't squeeze the Charmin.'"

I assumed she was joking until a few days later, when the teenage mother showed me her precious infant. "I named her Charmin,' like 'please don't squeeze the Charmin.'"

Classmates would soon be calling her "T. P." for short.

The only name worse than Charmin' in my experience comes from a tale told me by a country woman many years ago. People in her neck of the woods thought it quite classy to give a child, male or female, a French-sounding name beginning with "La."

But a father was really furious when he came home from World War II to find out that his wife had named their daughter Latrine!

"What's the name of your little girl?" asked the orderly who was assisting a new mother get into a car outside the hospital.

"Femally," she said proudly.

"What an unusual name. Why did you pick that?"

"I didn't. The nurses already had it on her bracelet: (Female) Harmon."

When a Missouri mama named her little girl Picha (pronounced Picka), she could never have dreamed that someday her daughter would marry a man whose last name was Bugger.

Another mother named her son Anthony Stephen.

Only when he was older did she realize why he was the butt of many a joke: their last name began with "S."

An Army family stationed in Japan sent their two daughters to a movie, while Mom went to the hospital to have their little sister. The older girls watched the same movie eight hours. The baby's legal name was the movie's title: "Tugboat Annie."

At a baby shower, some of us were discussing names, and one woman knew of a child named Savon Levin. "You know," she said, "like 7-11."

This tale came from Missouri: a little girl was born during Hurricane Alicia, and so her middle name became Alicia.

Fine. But did they have to choose as her first name Hurricane?

An employer in Roanoke, Virginia remarked one day that he had processed an application for a teenager named Remember September.

An acquaintance within hearing distance grinned. "I know her. And she has a sister named Monday Morning."

Husbands haven't changed much, huh? Here's a true tale from the Civil War era. Fellow-author Selby had an ancestor who served in the Confederate Army. His wife wrote to him, asking what she should name their son. She gave him 14 choices and even made rhymes out of the list. Her husband's reply was "That will be fine."

And so, this mother named her son Jonathan Jonas Solomon Saul Jeremiah Jacob Lazarus Paul Shadrach Simon Matthew Nat Timothy Pat.

Fran, a college friend, worked at the University of Virginia Hospital as a registrar. One of their patients, she told me, was named Queen Elizabeth Brown. "Imagine naming a baby that!" she exclaimed.

But that woman's name was not the oddest Fran encountered while at the UVA Hospital. Another patient had the first name General. Not only was he sick, but he had another problem.

He wanted to notify his family that his doctor was checking him into the hospital. He needed Fran's help to make the long distance collect call.

Seems the operator kept hanging up on him. Wouldn't believe an African-American man could really be General Stonewall Jackson.

Sometimes the naming process gets complicated.

Our friends, Robert and Jane, intended to name their little girl Kathleen after Jane's mother. But when they saw her those first hours, she always had her mouth open for food like a baby robin. They named her Robyn with a "y."

Grandma was not pleased. In fact, she hated that name. Despised it. Refused to call the baby anything but Kathleen Hargett (her maiden name). That was the double name that the Southern lady was certain they would have used, had they not had that moment of insanity while signing the birth certificate.

Fortunately for all of them, the two families lived several states apart. Holidays were difficult, though, for the name shame became a major obstacle to pleasant conversation.

By the time the child was four years old, her parents gave in. They paid the fee and legally changed her name to keep peace in the family. But they would call her Ilene.

Think of it! The preschooler had always answered to Robyn—or to Kathleen Hargett, when her grandparents visited. Now she, her kindergarten teacher, relatives and friends would have to get used to a third name, Ilene.

Can a little child have an identity crisis? An Ilene-ity crisis?

Although they named their son the first day he was born, Ellen wanted to think about it a few days. You see, she couldn't decide whether to discount her in-laws' wishes. They had planned to name him Pender. Her in-laws didn't like that at all.

"A county! Why would you name him for a county? And the poorest one in the state, at that!" they chided.

"That county was named for your ancestors!" huffed the new mother's mother.

Well, they compromised by making Pender the middle

name and then used a nickname and thought it was all settled. But about 62 days after the birth, Ellen remembered that she had only 60 days to change the name on the birth certificate. His legal name had already been filled: "Baby Boy Moffatt."

Just supposin'. . .

Let's call him "Seine!" suggested hubby.
"Fine," said the expectant mom, exasperated with the name game. "And if it's twins, the other one will be Insane."

Dad from Armenia bought an Armenian dictionary and name books. His wife, expecting soon, thumbed through them.
Well, she gave it the college try and thought she had found a really beautiful one. It had a lyrical sound. She later explained to friends, "If you could forget what it meant, it would really be nice to name her the word for nausea." She grinned, "It's even appropriate: that's what our first months together were like."

What about these whys?

"People ask us why we named our baby Kristen Katherine," said an adoptive mother, who had to go out of state to get the infant. "It's because we had just gotten to the Ks in the baby name book when our plane arrived in Texas."

Odessa's Saluda, North Carolina home was in a deep hollow within sound distance of the steepest railroad grade east of the Rocky Mountains. When Odessa's last-born boy child was due, she had long ago run out of names. Just as the early morning steam engine was huffing up the grade, Odessa was "birthin.'" It came to her! She would name him Local Freight. They called him "Local" for short.

Mothers seem to come up with the oddest ones when they wait until they get to the hospital to name their babies. One little girl was named Placenta.
Reckon the mama thought her doctor named her baby when she heard him say, "Placenta's coming out"?

22

NEW MOM, NEW BABE, NO INSTRUCTIONS

How-to manuals should come with infants. Ignorance is not bliss; it's terror.

Late in the evening of day four, an Atlanta mother was holding her son, Jake, who seemed to be wheezing, "He can't breathe!" Elaine said, rushing to phone the doctor. After a short deliberation, she hurriedly took Jake to the emergency room for treatment.

There the physician gently probed the dried mucus and cleared Jake's tiny nasal passages. In a soft voice, Doctor Wonderful said, "Older children usually get this stuff out with their fingers."

Elaine sighed, "My husband hasn't taught him to do that yet."

"My next door neighbor, whom I rarely see, appeared at my door with her three-week-old baby in one arm and two thermometers in her other hand," related Cindy, a young newlywed. "When she said her baby was hot and she didn't know what to do with the thermometers, my solution was to call 911."

We were as excited as our friends from law school over the new baby they had just adopted. My husband Randy and I arrived only hours after Mebane had entered the household. We took turns holding the tiny infant until she developed the hiccups. All four of us laughed at the cute sounds. But they didn't stop. Minutes were counted off in multiple hics. What must we do? None of us four college graduates had a clue. Remember the woman who had hiccups for 30 years? Poor Mebane! We must do something to make them go away. But what?

Marsha, Mebane's novice mom, rushed to the phone to call her next door neighbor, the mother of seven. She returned red-faced. "Nothing," she repeated. "Mebane will stop on her own."

An anxious first-time mother, Bet worried that the three tiny holes in the rubber nipple of the bottle were too small to let much formula through. Carefully, she heated a needle and enlarged the holes, only to have the milk pour out in choking streams. She ruined several nipples before surrendering to the urge to consult an authority.

"Dr. Walker," she asked, "just how important is it to get those holes the right size?"

He matched her serious tone. *"Extremely* important," he said, "with the *first* baby."

When Betty's firstborn, Andrew, was born Thanksgiving weekend, she and her husband became the typical germ-paranoid parents. In fact, although Betty's husband was a minister, they did not take Andrew to church until January.

On his first visit, they raced into the parking lot with their precious bundle, stopped right in front of the nursery door and ran inside.

Thirty minutes later, during the sermon, a nursery worker looked out the window and asked, "Isn't that the pastor's car sitting in the middle of the parking lot with the engine running and two of the doors standing open?"

Betty admits that her perspective on germs changed a bit:

"With Andrew, we didn't come out of the house for *weeks* after his birth.

"With Aaron, we didn't come out of the house for *days* after his birth.

"With Ellie, we stopped at the mall on the way home from the hospital."

A brand new mom called an Illinois Mother's Help Line and wailed, "It's six p.m. and I haven't gotten dressed yet!"

Born seven weeks premature in Colorado Springs, Buddy spent every minute hooked up to monitors and machines.

Finally, Theresa was allowed to hold her son. A nurse placed him into her arms, so that she could rock him. Theresa lovingly began humming a lullaby. Buddy noticed immediately. She could tell because he put both hands over his ears.

24

Holly and her husband were apprehensive about taking their newborn son to the movies. But Jimmy quietly drank his bottle, and Holly turned him onto her shoulder to burp him. That caused quite a disturbance—and not just because Jimmy shot geysers of formula at the people behind them. Holly had burped herself.

An almost-mom had heard of disposable bottles, but when her friend showed her a box of liners, her eyes nearly popped. "You mean there are 50 bottles in there?"

Her baby was only a few days old and the disposable diapers didn't seem to fit right. Candice called a trusted friend.

"Honey, the teddy bears go on the front," the friend said condescendingly.

A brand new mother, who was in the top management of a public radio station, was scheduled to meet a man who was going to give $20,000 to the station. Her boss walked in just before the meeting and spied two wet spots on the executive's blouse. Yep, telltale nursing circles.

Solution: the boss found another woman on the staff who was remotely her build and got them to switch blouses. Never mind the style or color.

Papas have problems, too.

New dads can be as inept as new moms. A few nights after baby came home to stay, Dad and Mom reversed roles for the wee-hours feeding. Dad was to do the job.

But the gallant guy stayed in the kitchen so long, Mama Bobbie got up to check on him. There he was, groggily warming a Pepsi bottle.

Their infant was screaming but wouldn't take his bottle. Mom was too sick to nurse him, but Dad got a great idea.

He donned her familiar bathrobe to fool his son into thinking he was Mom.

Didn't work.

Surprise! Siblings and other children don't read baby manuals either.

Awaiting a pediatrician appointment, Hannah, 2, was playing with two dolls in the waiting room. Patti watched as her daughter raised her shirt and placed one baby doll at each breast to nurse. To the one on the right, she said, "You can have milk." To the one on the left: "You can have apple juice."

Baby Joseph's big sister was horrified at breast-feeding time. "Mommy! He's eating your arm!"

"Mommy!" yelled Becca, 2. "Your bra's in the refrigerator!"
It was the baby's bottle with the breast pump cup still attached.

Darlene asked the nurse at the pediatrician's office if she could take her boys into the waiting room reserved for teens. The nurse stared at her. Darlene, who was a bit flushed, was holding her newborn, but there was no teenager in sight.
Then the nurse understood. A 2-year-old boy was racing around the room full of mothers with beautiful new babies. "Hit the baby!" he yelled at one. He stomped over to another. "Smash the baby!"

Bet's sons, ages 2 and 5, went next door together to see their newborn neighbor. When they returned, 5-year-old Andrew reported in wonderment, "Mommy, Mrs. Toney's baby is so new, it's still a girl!"

Kat used the accepted anatomical names when teaching vocabulary to their children ("urinate" not "pee pee," for instance).
When she brought her second child, Johnny, home from the hospital, his 3-year-old sister, Ginny, commented on every detail of his appearance. First, "He's red like my blanket." And later, as Kat was changing him, "He has a Johnny-talia, not a Ginny-talia."

TERRIBLE TWOS — TERRIBLE FOR MOM

You may dread this before it happens, but until your first child turns 2, you can't imagine what everyone else complains about.

My daughter was a little angel, fully living up to her name, Joy. She obeyed, never talked back, never even cried unless she was sick or hurt. Whining was not in our vocabulary.

The day she turned 2, the whine switch went on and the broken record began the "no" tune.

No, she did *not* want to go into the swimming pool. No, she didn't want to set foot in *any* water— or sand—or even grass. She'd scream if anyone tried to coax her. We were at the beach. For a week.

Sometimes, when Bonnie and her younger brother were both taking naps, Harriet would lie down from sheer exhaustion. Bonnie would check to see if her mother was asleep and then somehow lift the screen door latch and take off.

"The only way I could find her," said Harriet, "was to follow the clothes she removed on her flight to toddler freedom."

Finally, one afternoon, Harriet feigned sleep and followed her little adventurer. "I wanted to know how she was unlocking the hook that I had to stand on my tiptoes to reach," Harriet said. "She was getting the broom out of the closet at the top of the cellar steps, lifting the latch and returning the broom. This child was only 2!"

Harriet and her husband replaced the hook with one that had to be pulled back to open. Bonnie got out anyway. She would push a heavy lounge chair to the door and stand on the top of the back until she could open the latch. Of course, she pushed the chair back before taking off.

Harriet told of their next remedy. "We finally decided, to preserve my sanity, that we should put up a high fence in the backyard." She sighed, "As the men were installing it, Bonnie was climbing over it.

Stuart was supposed to be napping, but when Ashley, her mother, opened the door, two of the hinges were off. Stuart had unscrewed the tops and pulled the pins out. One top was nowhere to be found. She was holding the doorstop, which her mother didn't recognize at first until Stuart pointed to the hole in the baseboard. The wallpaper border, four feet from the floor, had been just the right height for Stuart to peel off while standing on her crib. As for the crib, it was upside down.

Maria's toddler was "into bugs" with great delight, so when Maria corralled a giant spider in the kitchen she called, "Mindy, Mindy, come here!" Meanwhile, Maria killed it with her husband's size 13 shoe.

As Maria lifted the shoe to show off the huge specimen, Mindy sniffed, "I'm not going to eat *that* one, 'cause he's dead."

Wendy was in a Pennsylvania discount store to pick up the essentials of babydom. She was checking the prices on formula by the case and left the shopping cart just for a moment. One of her twin sons, Max, was in the seat. Eli was in the basket. The cart was parked near a 20-foot-tall ball display.

Somehow, they quietly worked a hole in the wire encasement. It was just big enough to release all hundred or so balls out in a bouncing fury. Balls were hitting people on the head, knocking over displays, and giving other delighted children balls in their carts.

The store manager gave them a gift (two balls) to leave.

Tahirah's older sister was learning the importance of keeping her private parts private, so Shondra thought it would be a good idea to teach this lesson to 2-year-old Tahirah.

So after her bath, Shondra pointed out the area and said, "Private."

Tahirah repeated the new word.

Shondra explained that no one should touch that part, and they practiced several times.

Later that day, the child's father and grandparents came home and gathered in the living room. Tahirah stood in front of the television set, raised her dress, pulled down her panties and, in her proudest voice exclaimed, "Look! Private!"

For many a year, Gerri held the distinction in their Chesterfield, Missouri neighborhood for having the youngest kid ever brought home by the police. Gerri had been in her backyard with her daughter in a stroller and her dog on a leash when an officer drove up. "Lady, do you have a little boy?"

"Yes. He's right here," she replied glancing around for her son, Tommy, who had been riding his Big Wheel.

"I don't think so," he said. "We picked him up on another street. Maybe you'd better keep your son on a leash and let the dog run free."

A refined lady from their congregation came to call on Betty, a Chapel Hill preacher's wife, to deliver a gift for the new baby. Just as she was seated, Aaron, 2, climbed on her lap and greeted her in a uniquely gruff voice, "Hi, Butthead!"

Ashley had a sweet habit of always kissing little Stuart's hurts they called "boo boos." Only once did Ashley balk.

"Mama, kiss bot," said Stuart in a plaintive voice. She had a bad case of diaper rash.

Nan has a son who, at 2, was barred from shopping malls. While in an umbrella-style stroller, he would wiggle until his feet touched the floor then take off running with the stroller strapped to his back. He was a menace to shoppers and aisle displays. Nan sighed, "We didn't take him out in public again until he was 3."

Kimberly was determined that Brendan, who was almost 3, would learn to dress himself before his new sibling arrived. But no matter how hard he tried, there were always two or more items on backwards—shoes on the wrong feet, underpants backwards, shirt inside out, whatever. She suspected that he, "in typical male fashion," just didn't care.

"You'd think he'd have at least a 50-50 chance of getting it right once in a while," she said, "but no, morning after morning, he would come downstairs with almost everything on backwards."

Finally, Kimberly had a little talk with him about concentrating on what he was doing and noticing where the tags were. It sank in. The next morning, Brendan proudly came downstairs with everything on correctly. She was thrilled and told him so. Then she looked at his nursery school calendar. That day was Backwards Day at school!

Out of the corner of her eye, Jean saw James, who was wearing only a diaper, take something out of the refrigerator. Quick as a flash he ran to his room and shut the door. A moment or two later, she followed to see what he had taken. A tub of butter. And he had used it all to grease himself.

"I couldn't pick him up!" she said. "Ever heard of a greased pig?"

James kept slipping out of her grasp. Jean would catch him and James would slither away. She finally was able to grab him by the nape of his neck, kitty-style.

How can someone so little move so fast? In an instant, Hunter was throwing Janet's keys into the front yard. Her only key ring! She searched and searched. Never found them. Had to call Toyota to come make a new set.

It's the year of the pot.

One of the joys of the year between 2 and 3 is potty training. As one mom put it, "You have to ask them every 20 minutes or so if they need to go."

Robbye told about her own son, who loved to play with his toy cars in their back yard. His favorite "road" was a board along the edge of a fence his dad had built around the garbage cans. It was just out of sight from the kitchen window, but Robbye could usually hear him "rrrrrrr-ing" his car along that board.

One morning, the 20 minutes were up, and she hollered out the window, "Do you want to come inside and pee?"

A very puzzled garbage man peered around the corner, "No MA'AM!"

During a potty training feat, Corbin was sitting halfway in the toilet, swinging his legs, curling his toes, and allowing nature to take its course. A noise sounded below him, and Corbin proclaimed, "My butt just snored!"

Shopping at Sears, Maggie had been talking earnestly with a salesman. Annoyed by her daughter Amy's consistent pulling on her skirt, she ignored the child until the yanking stopped. When Maggie finally turned to look for her, Amy was walking back towards her, pulling up her shorts.

"Amy, what did you just do?"

Proudly, Amy pointed to a nearby toilet display and said, "I went to the bathroom all by myself, Mommy."

When Joy's little girl, Martha, was celebrating her second Christmas, her uncle sent her a Winnie-the-Pooh bear.

She finally got the big decorated box unwrapped and pulled out the putty-colored cuddly bear dressed in a bright teal sweater. Joy excitedly exclaimed, "Oh, it's Pooh!"

With that, Martha ran to the powder room, threw him into the toilet and flushed. Of course, the bathroom was soon flooded with a stuffed bear in the commode.

Martha, you see, was being potty-trained and thought Pooh was something else.

Gina had a very difficult time training Nicholas not to do "number two" in his pants. To encourage him, whenever he passed gas, she would say that his "dooks" were telling him that they needed to get in the potty.

One day, Gina was looking through videos at the public library in Spartanburg, South Carolina. Nicholas sat patiently beside her.

When flipping through the plastic video covers, one scraped against the holder. Nicholas, and undoubtedly the other patrons standing close by, heard the noise.

They also heard him ask, "You need to 'dook' in the potty, Mommy?"

Bonnie asked her sister-in-law, Theresa, to spend the night at their house so that she and her husband could go to an early morning appointment, leaving their boys behind.

The next day, Theresa reported being awakened by the family cat screeching as though being tortured.

She ran toward the sound and found 2-year-old Danny in the bathroom dunking the hind end of the kitten into the commode saying, "Go potty, Kitty! Go potty!"

Mom was having a group over for coffee that morning in the '60s. "Stay outside," she had told Tom, who was not quite 3. "And don't mess your pants."

Now think about this. What if...?

An obedient child, Tom got rather clever when the urge hit.

His mother didn't find out how clever until she saw that their milkman had left the bottles on the patio. Tom had pulled down his training pants and dropped one into the milk box just outside the front door.

You find out what it's like to be the mother of a 2-year-old when...

* You wake up at 4 a.m. and find the little darling pouring Parmesan cheese all over the kitchen.

* You go out with a friend and casually remark, "Oh look at the horsie."

* You discover that the labels have been torn off all the cans in the pantry and, for the next month, can't tell whether you're opening a can of peas or dog food.

* You find a red chalk line drawn from the top to the bottom of the stairway on the newly laid carpet. (The professionals swear that you cannot get red dye out, so you have to replace all the carpet on the stairs.)

* You realize that your child has a second sense about what you treasure the most. In Nan's case, it was a prize ceramic model of a house in England that they used to live in. Her son scaled tables, cupboards and shelving to reach it, only to drop and break it into 36 pieces.

* No crib sides, kiddie gate, dead bolt, live wire or chloroform will keep him in.

* Your extended family stops visiting.

* Your friends invite you to "adults only" parties.

* Your other children try whining to get their way.

* You wake up to the fact that she is saying "umbrella" while the rest of the family is still calling it a "bum-bum."

Think you've got problems? Consider the terrible twos times two—or more!

Nan from Houston describes double trouble:

"So how bad can it be? Incomprehensible for Moms with only one at that stage. They watch me take one from the car, set him down, chase after him as he runs into the path of an oncoming car, bring him back and threaten him with a fate worse than death. He laughs at me and runs right back out into the street again. If he stops a minute, I take the other one out, then I grab the first and take them indoors. To the casual observer, this is very funny and elicits cries of 'Look, twins, how cute!' as they watch me struggle bravely on.

"This performance gets repeated daily. I feel I have to take them out, because after two hours in the house, it is demolished and I am shattered. Sometimes, I take them for walks to a nearby park. That is also exhausting for me: Justin goes one way and Vincent goes the other. I call it the 'split mother syndrome.'

"Mealtimes. What can I say? Free-for-all. Major industrial disaster. Total chaos. Vincent's latest trick is to throw all his food on the floor, piece by piece, then put the bowl on his head. Justin has just learned to take the top off his cup and thinks it's just marvelous to pour his milk all over the table.

"In a former life, I used to work as a pediatric dietitian, counseling parents how to feed their children. I didn't believe the stories they told me. I do now.

"After nap time once, I went in to find that my boys had taken their closet clothes poles down and were Ninja fighting.

"Bedtimes. We moved them into beds because they were climbing out of their cribs. However, going to bed now takes on a whole new meaning. Unless one adult is willing to stay in the room until they fall asleep (which often takes an hour or more— and I, for one, do not have the patience for that), they refuse to settle down and sleep. They use the beds as trampolines. They empty every drawer in the room. They unfold diapers and disperse them around. They unload their toy box onto every square inch of floor. If one does manage to fall asleep, the other is right there to wake him up and continue playing. Several times a night, I go in and tuck them into bed, administering stern warnings. Several times a night, they giggle, climb out of bed and continue demolishing their room.

"Straight jackets—that's the answer. One for each of us."

Marie, mother of triplets, reports:
"Well as a matter of fact, today, I was just outside the kitchen door, tossing a ball back and forth with Michael, when I heard crashing noises in the kitchen. I looked in to find Meagan

and Janelle at the lazy susan, picking spice jars up and throwing them over their shoulders. The Tabasco bottle had hit the floor, the bottom fell out and there was Tabasco sauce everywhere."

A mother of triplets, Luanne, said, "There's nothing printable about what my girls did when they were 2." She told of entering their room one day after nap time. "They had taken off their diapers and smeared (you-know-what) all over the walls."

These same girls used to drag the mattresses off their beds and prop them against the headboard to make slides. They pulled out the drawers of their dresser to make steps to climb up on top.

Peggy, the mom of the only quads I know, remembers the church Halloween party when Curtis, Andrew, Rush and Mary Stevens, adorably dressed as four of the 101 Dalmatians, were frolicking atop the gym's bleachers. Suddenly a fire alarm was blaring. Parents and children turned to see four firehouse dogs standing below the alarm looking rather shocked. That incident caused the large suburban church to change the style of fire alarms within children's reach.

Two years later, the same church, because of the same children, dropped the Christmas Eve tradition of passing the light candle-to-candle, person-to-person, pew-to-pew. Somehow in the passing, Mary Stevens's pretty blond curls caught afire.

Oh, and which 2-year-old pulled the alarm? No one's talking. At 7, their motto is still "One for all and all for four."

And then there's Marguerite, mother of twins, now age 4, and triplets, 2. I phoned her to ask what it's like having three "terrible twos."

"People can't imagine," she sighed. "Right now, they're quiet. That means they're either in the toilet, sink or trash."

She recalled the day she caught #1 biting #2, who was biting #3, who was trying to get her teeth into #1.

And what happens when she takes them out?

"I use my handicapped sticker whenever I can," she confessed and then told me about the ordeal of moving into a new home with five under the age of 3. "Oh, oh, now they're into the cookies, and I'm not doing a thing about it."

That was my cue to hang up before the cookies ended up in the toilet, sink or trash.

SAID *WHAT?*

We could hardly wait for them to talk. Then we couldn't shut them up. But wasn't it fun when they were learning new words?

Our long-awaited newly-adopted child, Joy, stood at a footstool in our den, looking at her favorite picture book. She touched her finger to the cat on the cover and said, "Kit-ty."

"Did you hear that? Did you hear that?" my husband exclaimed, jumping up from his chair. "She said 'Daddy'!"

Carole and her family were worried. Her daughter, Jenny was a late talker (non-talker, to be more precise).

One day, Carole put a plate of food on Jenny's high chair tray. Jenny frowned. "You *know* I don't like that."

Sara was strolling her son, Rick, down a sidewalk when he came out with new words to warm her heart: "Mommy, I love you." She was basking in his adoration when he spoke again. "Car, I love you. Tree, I love you."

Several bright stars were visible one November evening in Pennsylvania when Lin emerged from a building with Megan, not quite 4. "Look!" said Megan, pointing skyward. "Uterus."

That hot summer day, the waiter brought drinks to the table, commenting about the sweat on their glasses.

"That's condensation," said 3-year-old Mikey.

The waiter was amazed that such a little boy had such a big vocabulary and said so.

Mom beamed.

Mikey puffed. "I'm not a little boy. I'm a big boy. I make pee pee and poop poop in the potty."

Fran and her husband introduced Scrabble into their Atlanta home in an attempt to spark an interest in spelling in their second grader. Predictably, Chrissy was less than thrilled.

Preschooler Will loved it. This unexpected fervor was fraught with numerous problems, not the least of which was Will's inability to read or spell. Minor details. In time, he had a repertoire of about ten words (cat, dog, mom, dad...). By placing them on a couple of those red and blue bonus squares, he became the quintessential high scorer.

One day, Fran was playing with him when, after stuffing popcorn into his mouth and drawing four new tiles, Will asked, "Mom, would you be upset if I used the 'F' word for my last turn. I know it's not a nice word, but I have all the letters."

Fran spewed her popcorn across the coffee table. "The 'F' word?" she asked. "Where have you heard that?"

"Car pool," he said. "Everybody knows it."

"Um...I don't know," she stuttered. "Tell me. What exactly is the 'F' word?"

"Oh you know," he said, leaning closer to her ear. "That word that means gas."

"Mama, the nurse checked us at school today, and I have no headlights," Carolyn's little girl said matter-of-factly.

No headlights? Did an eye test show that she needed glasses? A nurse from Webster City, Iowa, Carolyn could not imagine what else could be wrong. Then it hit her. No head lice.

Lynn's youngest daughter Stacey had been taking lessons at an aquatic club, learning basic strokes, floating and cannon-balling into the water. As Lynn and Stacey arrived at preschool one morning, Stacey announced to her teacher, "I have an ear confection from doing candy balls in the pool."

A teacher in Anchorage, Alaska, was curious when her pre-schooler came home with the question, "Do we have harmon-ica?"

"No, we don't. You mean the musical instrument?"

"No, no," he said, frustrated. "Do we DO harmonica? We do Christmas..."

Suddenly, the mother understood and began explaining how Jewish people celebrate Hanukkah. When she finished, she asked, "Do you have many Jewish boys in your class?"

"Oh no," he replied. "They're all from Anchorage."

Pleased that Rachael had a good grasp of phonics, Tracy, who is from Lansdale, Pennsylvania, suggested that her little girl write a letter to Santa one December evening.

They chattered away while Tracy was fixing dinner, sounding out words and laughing about what Rachael wanted.

"Will you mail this for me, Mommy?" she asked, after drawing a big heart on the envelope.

"Of course," Tracy replied, putting it on the counter. It wasn't until the next morning that she noticed how her child had addressed the letter: "To Satan."

Sometimes, they surprise us...

When Lidewey's son Noah was all of 4 years old, he already had an extensive vocabulary and strong personality. One day, his mother said something to inflame his anger. He stomped over to her and with his hands on his hips, looked her straight in the eye and yelled, "Mommy, you are so stup..."

At that point, Lidewey gave him "the look" which stopped him dead in his tracks.

A silent pause later, Noah concluded with, "pendous!"

His parents had been telling their 8-year-old David how great camp would be. His mother, Jane, kept saying it would be the most fun he ever had.

She could hardly wait to open his first letter. It said: "Dear Mom: This is the worst fun I've ever had! COME AND GET ME!"

Ann struggled with what to say to her 3-year-old daughter who repeatedly stimulated herself whenever she took a bath. What if little Anna did that in front of her grandparents?

One night when Anna was at it again, Ann said, "There's nothing wrong with doing that, and I know it feels good. But you should only do that in privacy—when you're by yourself."

Anna pondered a moment. "Well, I guess you'd better leave then."

Janet is doing what countless other mothers have said "we're gonna do" or "we should've done." She keeps a journal of her daughters' wee quotes and wisdom. Here are a few:

Jamie, age 2: "Mommy send $2 tomorrow to school. I'm going to make you a tie for Mother's Day."

Samantha (Sammy), age 4: "God knows what you do, even when He's not looking."

Sammy, age 4: "If I say I don't want to kiss you, what I mean is it takes a little while for my heart to make them."

Sammy, 4, at bath time: "Mommy, I bet you can't dance as good as me naked in high heels!" (Husband's response: "Oh, give it a try, Mom!")

Benjamin, 4, asked, "Mom, would you like a pet?"

"Well, no," Nan replied. "Would you?"

"Sure. We could have a dog or a cat or a goldfish. Which would you like, Mom?"

"I would like a goldfish."

"Well, I would like a cat."

"But we can't get a cat," Nan sighed. "Papa is allergic to cats."

"What's allergic?"

"It means that cats make him sneeze and feel miserable."

"Okay, Mom, I'll tell you what," Ben said thoughtfully. "We'll get a cat, and Papa can move out."

This kid was old enough to know better. A young man in the 1930s, Robert rang the doorbell at his girlfriend's house and asked her mother if he could go up to her room, a shocking request in those days. The mother was stunned but nodded.

He bounded upstairs and opened Alice's top drawer. Turning to his future mother-in-law, he explained. "My mother says a top dresser drawer tells what kind of housekeeper a girl will be."

Two University of Michigan grads (and loyal fans) had married and moved to the South with their daughters, Dottie and Gail.

One night at dinner, something miffed 5-year-old Gail. She glared at her mother and said, "I don't love you, I don't love Daddy and I don't love Dottie!"

They did not drop dead. They kept on eating.

42

So Gail rolled out her big gun. "And," she added, "I don't even want to go to Michigan!"

befuddle us...

Tired from a hard morning of housework, Jeannine was taking a few minutes to lounge outside, when her 10-year-old Devin interrupted asking for chocolate milk. She told him to make it himself. The recipe was on the box.

First he called out the kitchen door to find out where the measuring cup was. Then he couldn't find the cocoa. Just when Jeannine thought he must have all the ingredients assembled, he yelled out once more. "Do we have any yield? I need two cups."

Ann had taken Terry, 3, along when she stopped by their church to help the priest prepare for Lent.

A little later at home, she noticed that Terry was limping. Ann reached for her foot and saw that the laces had been tied so tightly that the sneaker was cutting off Terry's circulation. She frowned, "Who tied your shoe?"

"God did it."

and, yes, frustrate us!

Carole of St. Charles, Illinois, was driving car pool for three rambunctious pre-school boys, who seemed to be experimenting with how many times they could use the word "penis."

Carole finally lost her patience."That's enough 'potty talk'!" she ordered. Then she resorted to the fine art of distraction. "Look at that man on the roof. He sure is high. I hope he doesn't fall."

One of the boys responded, "Yeah, he might really hurt his penis!"

Sally and Ginny were having coffee at Ginny's house while their 6-year-old sons were playing in another room. All of a sudden Ginny's son, Gene, came tearing into the living room, yelling, his playmate in pursuit. Gene ran right into Ginny's antique stand, knocking her great-grandmother's teacups a'flying. Ginny jumped up to see all the china broken and the stand in two jagged pieces. Gene saw her stricken face and soothed, "Hey, Mom, don't WORRY! I'm okay."

James really enjoyed repeating a new word he learned on the playground. He was feeling a new sense of power from the reaction to "Butthead."

While the family was driving to dinner his mother, Mary, was trying to explain that it was "not nice."

His father was backing her up when James retorted. "You say butt, Daddy."

Mary's husband smiled. "Yes, like *but* it's time for you to take a bath. Or, *but* I have to go to the store."

James looked perplexed. "*Butthead*, I have to go to the store now."

What's a mother?

Houston mother Kate and her son, Patrick, 3, were admiring his baby sister. He cocked his head in thought. "I wonder what Claire will be when she grows up."

"I don't know," said Kate, "but I hope she grows up to be happy."

Patrick looked over at his mother. "You grew up to be... nothing!"

Which is harder? For us to communicate our faith? Or for our children to understand it?

One evening, Judy told 5-year-old Kim to pick up her toys from the den floor and take them to her toy box on the back porch. Knowing that this involved a trip down a long, dark center hall, she added, "Don't be afraid. Jesus will go with you."

Kim thought a minute, then looked up with intent green eyes. "Well," she said, "if he's going, why can't *he* take 'em?"

Peggy overheard her not-yet-3-year-old saying her prayers alone in her crib. "God bless everyone. God make me pretty. And gosh darn it—because we don't say 'God damn #@*.'"

"Excuse me?" interrupted Peggy from the other room.

A surprised voice called back, "Hey! You can't see me!"

44

At bedtime, Maybelle's 6-year-old William was saying his prayers aloud. He stopped to ask if it were okay for him to ask God to bless his class.

"That would be fine," Maybelle told him.

"I don't like everybody, so I'll just go by their numbers." he said. (Each child in his Clinton, Mississippi school is assigned a number at the beginning of the year.) "Bless number 1, bless number 4, bless number 7..."

Marianne from Feasterville, Pennsylvania knew that Paul was having a test about guardian angels in his first-grade religion class, so as they were driving to school, she decided to quiz him to be sure he understood the material. "Who is it that watches over you and guards you all day?" she asked.

Paul thought a moment before he answered, "Nicholas!"

As in Saint? No. Nicholas is his best friend who knows karate.

Anna's daughter Betsy was riding home from Sunday school with her aunt Sally.

"What was your Bible story about this morning?"

"Cowboys," replied the 3-year-old.

"Are you sure the subject was cowboys?"

"Yes," came the emphatic reply. "We learned all about a sheriff named Jesus and his posse."

At Christmastime, their church called one of their services "Jesus's Birthday Party."

As the choir began singing, Ben, 5, began crying. He was sniffing and sucking as only a broken-hearted child can do.

"What's wrong?" his mother wanted to know.

"It's Jesus's birthday," he bawled, "and he's not even here!"

Just then, the priest stepped forward.

Ben smiled. "There he is."

The assistant pastor asked Mindy how she liked church.

"Fine. I especially like the Halloween song and when you pass around the pizza crust."

Halloween song? Maria and the pastor wondered over that

one until Mindy sang out, "Praise Father, Son and Holy Ghost."

But the pizza puzzle took a bit longer.

"You mean the communion?" her mother asked.

"No, no. When you pass around the pizza crust."

Then Maria thought of their after-church coffee time and commented that they didn't have pizza then.

"No, no. It's when you say, 'May the pizza crust be with you,' and everybody shakes hands."

As she was giving Michael 5, his daily early morning cuddle, Judi said, "You're an angel from heaven. God sent you to me."

Michael looked up at her quizzically. "In the mail?"

Jane's family knew the local people who made and packaged liver mush. Her grandchildren had all been to the packing plant to watch the process. She thought it a fine educational outing until she heard a grandchild saying the Lord's Prayer. He asked God to "Deliver mush from evil."

A seasoned citizen, Elizabeth tells of teaching the Beatitudes in a children's Sunday school class during the 1950s. "Blessed are the meek," she said.

The preacher's son's hand shot up. "My mother is really blessed. She wears hers around her neck every Sunday."

Thelma was helping her son, Kit, go over the catechism. "How many sins are there?" she asked.

"Two," he replied. "Mortal sins and convenience sins."

Noah Webster should have heard these!

Irene of Yorkville, Illinois told of a holiday season when she and son, Sean, spent the day putting up the Christmas tree and other decorations. Irene was not feeling well.

By the end of the day, his hyperactivity was getting to her. She finally yelled, "Sean, do you know what PMS is?"

Sean had quickly replied, "That spells 'be quiet.'"

"I guess his father trained him on that one," said Irene.

46

A billboard depicting busty, big-haired female entertainers kept catching Fran's 6-year-old daughter's eye whenever they drove on the expressway near their Atlanta home. "Who are those women, Mommy? she'd ask. "Are they Barbies?"

"No," Fran would say. "Barbie isn't real. They aren't Barbies."

"Are they movie stars?"

Fran tried to deflect her questioning but couldn't get her to drop the subject. Finally, in desperation, she fumbled around and told her they were women who earned money by having very beautiful bodies.

"Oh, I get it," she said. "They're BOOBIE stars."

On the night before Paul was to start first grade, Marianne gave him a little talk about the proper names for bodily functions, in case he should ever need to tell the teacher. Lesson completed, she asked, "Now Paul, you know what BM means, right?"

"Sure," he replied. "Body manure."

So how come...?

Janie, age 6, rushed into the house breathless. "Mama! Jesus is coming!"

"How do you know?"

"Daddy was out working on the car and called to him."

Seated in the kitchen, Lisa's son, Daniel, 3, was struggling to get his boots off. "Shit, Shit, Shit!" he yelled.

She ran into the room to correct him. "Why did you say those three ugly words?" she asked with a frown.

He looked up innocently. "That's what Daddy says when he gets mad."

Cliff is not quite 3, according to Grandma Cary Ellen. When he wants to go outside, he says, "Owsi. Open dough-ah." At lunch: "Want mo-ah."

Where does he get that accent? she wondered.

Later, at play with Cliff, Cary Ellen says, "Pick that up off the flo-ah."

One day while Elizabeth, 3, was supposed to be napping, her mother, Susan, overheard her walk up to her baby monitor and say, "Hamburgers and french fries, please."

Quirky questions:

Betty had to ponder this from Aaron, who asked with great concern, "Mom, what would you do if a robber threw up on your shoes?"

Phyllis took Craig, who was 4, to see his grandfather, who had just come home from the hospital after a double hernia operation.
Craig began going from room to room on both floors of the house. He came back downstairs with a very perplexed look on his face. "Well where is it?" he wanted to know.
Neither Phyllis nor the other family visitors knew what he was looking for. "Where's what?" his aunt asked.
"The new baby!"
Everyone Craig knew who had been to the hospital had brought home a baby.

At 10, Jack, the oldest of four, came home from his parochial school in Edgecomb, Maine and went straight to his mother. "Teacher told us today that there's no Santa Claus," he said.
"What do you think?" Mary wisely asked.
"Well, I kinda knew about it," he said. "Moms go out shopping a lot." He pondered a moment. "But who's the guy in the red suit that brings the presents?"

Clare's father had shaved off his handlebar moustache. Little Clare wandered into her parent's bedroom early one morning while they were still half asleep. She looked puzzled when she pulled on her mother's arm. "Is that our father?"
Her mother smiled. "I hope so."

Her sons, ages 3 and 5, were seated on the sofa shaking when her husband walked in. Sandy was banging pots and pans in the kitchen.

"What's wrong with you?" he asked gingerly.

"I've got PMS, okay?" she nearly shouted. Actually, she had a bad case of motherhood, but a real malady was easier to explain.

A little later, the 5-year-old tiptoed in and asked in a gentle voice, "Would it hurt your PMS if I watch *The Sound of Music*?"

More questions, questions, questions:

Ever noticed how little children who barely know how to talk can make you feel downright dumb? They ask a simple question and all you can do is stammer, stutter or stare. Well, what would YOU say, if your kid asked:

"How come I'm me?"

"Why is ice cold?"

"What's inside my skin?"

"What does the tooth fairy look like?"

"Is Grandma going to cut new teeth?"

"Mommy, what kind of underwear does God wear?"

"Does God poot?"

"Why do you sit down to pee pee?"

"How did the baby in your tummy get stuck in there?"

"Why do I have to sleep alone, when you can sleep with Daddy?"

Harriet has a *mother's* question to ask: "If Dr. Spock was so smart, why didn't he give us the answers in his book?"

Kids really do say the darndest things, especially to other people, when Mom is around to turn red.

Her little girl was nearly 5, when Lindy, a divorcee, began dating again. A brand new boyfriend was at the house one evening when snow was falling.

The child noticed that it was coming down hard. She turned to the date sympathetically, "Don't drive home in the snow. Stay here! Mommy has a BIG bed."

"Mom can't come to the phone," said Tracie's son Drew, 4. "She's on the toilet."

True. Tracie was standing on the commode, cleaning the medicine cabinet.

After the noontime kindergarten car pool run, Bet decided to treat her 5-year-old son, Shepherd to a hot dog and milkshake at the lunch counter at Roses.

Shep, unaware that few people ask grace aloud in public, went into his customary "God is great, God is good..." routine, and even the waitress paused reverently in her tracks.

Bet basked sanctimoniously in the murmur of approval from nearby diners, until Shep followed his closing "amen" by clinking his milkshake glass against hers and pronouncing distinctly, "Well, cheers, Mom!"

Warren, at age 5, was a devoted thumb-sucker. His mother had done everything she could think of to stop his habit. Finally, she came up with the threat, "If you keep sucking that thumb, someday you'll blow up and burst."

She was pleased with the effectiveness of her white lie until the day that she and her son were waiting at a street corner for a light to change. A very pregnant woman was standing beside them. Warren looked at the stranger curiously. He walked around one side to get a better glimpse, they glanced up at her shyly and said, "I know what YOU'VE been doing!"

The preacher seemed to be enjoying Sunday dinner at their Georgia home when Maggie's youngest daughter, Peggy, came in from the kitchen, carrying a cup. She walked over to their minister and said politely, "Would you please spit in this cup?"

Puzzled, he asked why.

"Well," Peggy replied, "Mama says you're full of holy spit, and I want to see how full of holes your spit really is."

It was the late '60s, when older women still went shopping downtown in hats and gloves. In an effort to expose her son, Zane, to some "social graces," Sue took him to lunch in a fine department store tea room.

Within minutes, a close friend of Sue's mother-in-law was seated with another lady at a table beside them. The friend immediately recognized Zane, and they exchanged pleasantries.

Sue was proud of her well-behaved child, until he suddenly fingered the tablecloth, held it up high and frowned. "What's this?"

In the '90s, this might be shrugged off. But in the '50s, a mother of 6-year-old twins was mortified when she found out what one of them said at school. He hurried into his first grade classroom to announce, "We have a new sister, Elizabeth Ann! Now Mommy and Daddy are going to get married!"

Not true. They had been married for many years. Daddy was a preacher.

When Ann's son was about 3, she took him with her to have the car's oil changed. At the time, he liked to repeat dialogue from storybooks Ann had read to him. That's *exactly* what he was doing when he approached another patron in the waiting area and asked, "Who are you and where are you going to bite?"

Christine was shopping with 2-year-old Suzanne, when the child abruptly pointed to a male shopper and cried out in horror, "Mommy, that man is going to die!"

A psychic at age 2? No, Christine and her husband had done a really good job instilling an anti-smoking attitude in their children. The gentleman had a cigarette in his mouth.

A classy woman of the FFV (first families of Virginia) variety, Sharon was shopping in an elegant boutique with her 4-year-old daughter, Sue. The youngster passed gas.

Women shoppers nearby turned in their direction.

Sue looked up at her mom. "Excuse YOU!"

At her first teacher's conference with her son's kindergarten teacher, Charlotte heard about all of Chuck's virtues.

Chuck, who had been playing at the other end of the room, turned to the teacher as they were leaving. "I told you my mother was nice," he said, "even if she does dye her hair and has false teeth."

While riding in a car with their children, Elizabeth's friend asked Kyle, Elizabeth's 6-year-old son, what he liked best that his mother cooked. Her child had just named a sophisticated dish.

Kyle replied quickly, "McDonald's."

When he was 4, Jimmy's parents took him with them on a trip to Washington, D.C. It was the adventure of his short life: the Air and Space Museum, National Zoo, all the monuments and other "gift to the nation" sites.

So when he got home, what did he tell his grandmother that impressed him the most?

"The zoo's chimpanzee! He picked his nose and ate it!"

Soaking lazily in a bathtub was a luxury Marcelle of Falls Church, Virginia had forgone soon after her twins were born. A quick, efficient shower sufficed.

At bath time one evening when Marcelle was entertaining company, Ward began balking that he was old enough to take a shower. Marcelle had ignored him and returned to her guests in the living room when he rushed in. "Mom," he asked, "how come you never take a bath?"

The daughter of an NFL player, Tiara was dressed in a tiny cheerleader costume. A real cheerleader stepped up to coo, "Hello. Are you going to be a cheerleader when you grow up?"

"No,..." said the adorable child with cornrows ending in long, soft braids, "I'm going to be a doctor. My mommy says cheerleaders are clueless."

While the young woman was contemplating that, Stephanie jerked her child's hand. "Come on, Tiara. Where's your mother?"

Even when Mom isn't around...

Cynthia was worried that her daughter wouldn't talk at all on her first outing with her godmother. Allison, at 4, generally did not carry on a conversation with anyone. Cynthia walked her out to the car and warned me about the likely silence. As a godmother with no children yet, I wondered if I were taking her away from her mother too soon.

But the moment the car door slammed, Allison's motor-mouth turned on full speed. "You know what?"

"What, Allison?"

"My daddy took David and me to the ABC store, and you know what?"

"What, Allison?"

"He didn't buy us an ABC book."

Virginia, whose children were in a parochial school, lamented to a friend. "I can't go to the next PTA meeting."
"Why not?"
She explained that a sister told the children in Sandra's class to do something nice for their mothers. She had suggested that they fold down Mama's bed and lay her nightgown out.
Then Sandra had announced, "My mama doesn't wear anything to bed."

"My husband and I always kid around when the phone rings and someone hangs up," said Susan. "We say it was either a girlfriend or boyfriend."
One day, when Susan went to pick up her daughter, Janie, age 8, from school, Janie's teacher stepped into the hall.
"Is everything all right at home?" she had asked.
Of course, Janie had told her teacher that "Daddy's girlfriend kept calling last night."

Occasionally, mothers must ponder what *other* folks say.

New York City was an awesome sight for Katherine and her three teenage daughters, as they waited for a friend on the sidewalk outside the Port Authority building at 5 p.m. on a hot afternoon. Standing shoulder to shoulder with their backs pressed against the bus station wall, the four Southerners were wide-eyed at the sea of humanity rushing by.
A sharp-looking young girl hurried past them, paused, turned back and stopped. "Don't you know you can't turn a trick all bunched up like that? You got to spread out!"

Once in a while, a mom gets in the last word.

At the dinner table, Barbara was picking up her food with her hands.
"Don't eat with your fingers," her ma instructed as usual.
But Barbara had an answer this time. "Fingers were made before forks."
Ma didn't flinch. "Yours weren't."

DID *WHAT?*

Kids do the unexpected. That's what makes mothers' lives interesting—and gives them something to talk about.

This mother did not find out until years later that her 6-year-old daughter and 3-year-old son liked to play in the bathroom sink with her diaphragm. Now and then she had noticed that the powder seemed to have been washed off and would ask, "Have you two been playing with my little cup?"
"No, ma'am," they'd reply innocently.
But that's why they used to take turns drinking out of it.

Her 7-year-old son, Andy, had a friend over to play. Every mother knows that when it gets quiet, it's time to check. Susan found the door to his room closed and locked. She knocked, and there was a jangling of belt buckles. "What's going on?"
"Nothing. Just a minute," said son Andy.
"Why don't you want me to come in?"
"Hold on, we're coming."
"I was a kid once. What are you doing?"
"If you were a kid once, you KNOW what we're doing."

Her sister-in-law, a Yankee fuddy-duddy cleanliness nut would visit soon. Intent on making a good impression, Sue hired professional cleaners to spiffy up her house from floor to ceiling.
Just before Sis was to arrive, Sue went out. When she returned, Bitsy, her 8-year-old daughter, was wiping off the sliding glass door to the patio.
"I just had that done," said Sue.
"It just needs some shining," Bitsy said, rubbing the glass.
Sue walked down the hall to the bedrooms and noticed a wet spot on the carpet. How strange. Later, she went out on the patio and saw a bucket of horse manure. Aha! "Bitsy, did you bring your pony into the house?" she asked.
"Yes, Mama," said the petulant child. "I just wanted him to see where I sleep."

Betty recalls the day her family was introduced to their new neighborhood. She had just returned from the grocery store to find her husband quite contrite. He was supposed to have been watching their sons, Jimmy, 4, and Tommy, 2. He hadn't been paying attention.

Their "new kids on the block" had found some of their daddy's homemade blackberry wine and served it to assorted neighborhood kids, ages 2 to 5.

Every one of them went home tight.

While talking with her sister-in-law long distance, Maria was abruptly interrupted. The line went dead. She moved toward the wall where the phone was connected. There stood 3-year-old Brett, holding a handful of wires next to a gaping hole in the plaster.

"You talked too long," he said, "so I hung up on you."

Jean stepped into her living room. Someone's been murdered! she thought. Then she spied son James, 4, who'd filled his fireman's hat with ketchup and splashed it onto her rug, couch, walls and ceiling fan. The fan was swishing it high and low.

Both 5-year-old boys were swinging in the freezing cold with their pants and underwear around their shoes. By the time Mom got outside, they were leaning over, staring at themselves. Their explanation? "Just wanted to see what the cold would do."

A Topanga, California mom was awakened by her 4-year-old and 19-month-old gently tickling on her back. How sweet.

But a little later, she passed a mirror. Blood? A terrible disease? Her back was pocked and streaked. Then she saw the top to her best red calligraphy pen.

David, 4, was waving goodbye from the front porch. His baby sitter was seated on a step below him. He was really mad that his parents and older sister were leaving him behind. Just as Mom, Dad and Sis were backing out the driveway, he figured out a great way to get them to stay home with him. He peed on the baby sitter's head.

Vivian and her 2-year-old were watching television until Vivian fell asleep. She awoke with a start, a pang of guilt and heart-pounding panic. Little Rachel was gone and all was quiet.

Racing from room to room, Vivian was at once relieved to see Rachel safe. She had been very busy in the bathroom with some new stickers: a whole box of her mother's sanitary pads. Rachel had pulled off the tabs and stuck 20 pads on the walls, cabinet doors, toilet top, tub, everything within her reach.

What's a mom to do? At a mere 15 months, a Longview, Texas, child buried her dog, sat on the hole and lied about it.

Somehow, Star, the Shih Tzu survived.

So did this nameless kid.

A Grand Rapids mother wondered what they were teaching in kindergarten when her little girl built a snowman. He was anatomically correct.

All the children had been told never to play with the new power stapler. But Denise, age 12, just couldn't stand the curiosity. While her mother was out, she had examined it and turned it upside down.

When her parents drove up, there she was sitting on the front porch white as a ghost's sheet. Denise had to admit her transgression to get free.

Her thumbs were stapled together through the nails.

Janis caught her 3-year-old son coming out of his teenage sisters' bathroom with a cigarette pressed tightly between his lips. Oh, good, it wasn't a real cigarette. It was a tampon applicator.

When Steve was "eightish," he found a bird's nest cradling an egg. Nancy, his mother, allowed him to try incubation with a lamp in the bathroom. But she was unaware that he got up in the night to check on it.

Finding the bulb burned out, he took the bird's egg under his wing—literally. The youngster returned to bed and tucked the egg into his armpit. That might have worked if he hadn't sneezed.

A Philadelphia mom with six kids, ages 10 and under, walked into the kitchen to discover one of her middle children, a twin, splashing milk on the toddler's head. She gasped, "What are you doing?"

"Pouring milk," he said calmly, emptying the container on his giggling sister. "She *likes* it."

Away from home, life gets even more interesting.

"I'm a pacifist. When I had my first son, I was determined that we'd have no guns in our house," said Allison, mother of two boys. "But I've decided that if they don't have them, boys would make them out of toast."

One Sunday morning, as they were headed from the car to the church, she spied Benjamin, 2, with a toy gun. "How did you get that out of the car without my seeing you?" she asked.

Just then, they met the minister who was preaching that morning. "Oh, no," she thought.

But the minister pulled the Good Book from under his arm and made like it was an Uzi. Benjamin jumped behind a bush for the all-out shoot-out. Tyler, her 5-year-old, defended his brother with his finger.

Then along came a 90-year-old man. Allison froze with the thought, "Oh, wow, he'll be really upset."

With that, the seasoned citizen cocked his umbrella and "shaca, shaca," lasered them all dead.

Pamela called her 4-year-old son her "yellow-breasted buy-me bird." Everywhere they went, he would ask for things: a t-shirt, circus toy, etc. until her money or patience ran out. Then he would get teary-eyed and whine, "I never get anything."

Before heading for Disneyland, Pamela remedied the situation by telling him that she would buy him only one thing.

Mid-afternoon the first day, he raced to her. "I found it!" He pointed to a brass elephant taller than he was. Price: $200.

Rena had taken her son, Matthew, 4, to a South Carolina hospital for the pre-op tests before his tonsillectomy.

A nurse directed the procedures. "You can go right in there and pee-pee in this cup," she said, pointing the way to the men's room.

Matthew took the cup and pushed the door open. He soon returned, but the cup was empty.

Rena asked, "Son, what's the matter: could you not go?"

"Sure," said Matthew, "but there were toilets in there."

For a PTA program, a 5th grade square dance, Robbye had dressed her son in a plaid flannel shirt, a bandanna and jeans. But when she took him to the classroom, the teacher's face fell.

"Where's your white shirt, Vance?"

"Oh," he said furtively glancing at Robbye. "I forgot."

The teacher was eyeing Mom's white blouse. So what does a good mother do? Trades tops, of course. Her tailored shirt was passable for the performance. But this mother is not exactly petite. She could barely button Vance's shirt across her chest. The sleeves hung just below her elbows. Furthermore, red plaid didn't go with her outfit at all.

And so, Robbye slunk to a back row and shrunk in her seat, hoping that no one else in the PTA would notice her.

They did.

In our house, each person is allowed three foods he or she can dislike. I promised I would never serve any of the hated foods to the "hatee." That worked fine until we went to the beach with another family.

Although we had somewhat different dislikes, we all agreed on one: slithery, smelly oysters. The entertainment for the beach weekend was an afternoon of oystering. Of course, the main course of the dinner meal was those steamed gray slime blobs.

I got the whispered, "Do I have to?" from Joy and had to invoke my general rule of "you have to try everything on your plate" for this occasion.

At dinnertime, I brought out my contribution, our favorite strawberry gelatin salad. Joy was delighted. But our friends' middle child, Anna, was not.

"Eeeuuuuu! Red Jell-o! Who likes that?" she snarled.

Well, we were glad to have it. My husband was politely eating the oysters, but for every one that went into his mouth, another went into my hand to get rid of. Joy dutifully obeyed and ate one. I struggled to swallow what I truly regard as nasty, but only a few times.

Late that night, we were awakened by screams and cries coming from the girls' room. For the first time ever, Joy was sharing a bed with another child. She and Anna were both howling. Joy had thrown up all over Anna's bed. We mothers rushed in and flicked on the light. Pink vomit stenched the room.

Anna shouted, "I knew it! I knew it! It was the red Jell-o!"

Once in a while, a child acts smarter than the adults.

On a vacation trip from Waukegan, Illinois to York, Pennsylvania, a large family checked into a Sandusky, Ohio hotel mid-trip. The clerk summoned Chris, the mother. "Your daughter's been calling you," he said.

One of her six, 10-year-old Marissa, had gotten out of their car at a Burger King along the Indiana Turnpike and announced, "I'm going to ride with Uncle Aaron."

Fifteen minutes further down the road, the car Chris was riding in had a flat tire. "Where's Risa?" Uncle Aaron asked, when he stopped to help out.

"Aaron, stop playing," said Chris. "You know she's riding with you."

Tire replaced, they continued the trip.

And where was Marissa now?

The resourceful child had called everyone she could think of: her grandmother, her aunt, their pastor, the hotel. And she had befriended a truck driver, who gave her $100 to get home. The pastor called a friend, Sister Pearl, who had, by the time Marissa's family arrived in Sandusky, returned her to Waukegan.

Of course, Uncle Aaron was designated to drive the all-night trip with Dad to retrieve the child. Chris had a hard time understanding why Aaron hadn't realized she was missing 15 minutes from the Burger King.

Aaron shrugged. "I thought she was hiding."

Mommy's little helpers:

Exhausted from shining her great room floor with paste wax and elbow grease, Barbara was relaxing outdoors when son Todd, 3 announced he was going in to the bathroom.

A little later, Barbara checked on him. There he was on her shiny floor.

"I'm helping Mommy wax," he announced, beaming.

Todd had re-done almost the whole floor with the bacon grease he had found beneath the sink.

Kay was in the kitchen when 5-year-old Sarah entered holding a pair of pliers and something round. "It took me a long time," Sarah said with pride. "But I finally got it off." She held up the TV knob, permanently broken.

Kids will be kids, no matter what the decade.

Back in the early '50s, Elizabeth was hanging out some clothes in her Allentown backyard, when she heard Lois, her 4-year-old, lock the back door. Then she could hear water rushing across the kitchen floor. Lois had pulled the hose out of the old wringer washer and was spraying the floor.

During the '50s, a mother was getting the laundry out of the dryer with the dubious help of her 1-year-old. The child was amusing herself with a sanitary napkin belt.

Mother hoisted the tot onto her hip and slung the elastic belt around her neck so she wouldn't lose it in the pile of clothes she was carrying. Just then, the doorbell rang. She put down the clothes to open the door for a delivery man. And she tried to act nonchalant, hoping he wouldn't notice that her child was snapping an elastic Kotex belt on her neck.

Jane and her husband were entertaining his pilot colleagues and their wives in their Memphis home in the mid-1940s. The adults were talking in the living room when their 3-year-old Mike interrupted. "Mama can I play telephone with these?"

One of her flesh-colored foam rubber falsies hung from his ear. The nipple of the other one drooped from his mouth.

Good thing ALL children aren't like these!

From her very first month, Harriet's daughter Bonnie was determined to have her own way.

Every day was a challenge. She hated to be dressed. Just getting a diaper on her was a fight to the finish, and after a fumble with safety pins, Harriet's blood often soiled the cloth. Bonnie kept her clothes on for only a few minutes after she was put into her playpen. Everything went over the side, including her ribbons.

"A born nudist," complained Harriet during distress calls to her mother, who lived in a nearby Baltimore neighborhood.

Just before their second child, Ricky, was born, the family moved into a two-story house. Bonnie was not yet 2. Within 15 minutes, she got her head caught between iron railings outside, tumbled down the stairway indoors, and fell again, skinning both knees. "Believe me, having the hell scared out of you can bring on a baby!" said Harriet. "I called Mother to come get her."

One morning a few months later, Harriet went downstairs to get a bottle for Ricky and was greeted by the worst mess imaginable. She described it with a wrinkled nose. "My little bandit had taken all the eggs, a bottle of French dressing and a few boxes of chocolate pudding and tried to mix them all together. The slimy combination was still dripping off the kitchen table onto the chairs and the floor I'd washed just a few hours before. Chocolate fingerprints were everywhere. It was nauseating. Bonnie had climbed back into her crib, so her room was a mess, too."

Bonnie's explanation: "I baked you a cake."

Harriet immediately called her mother to come get Bonnie.

Not too long after that, Harriet heard Ricky crying. They were in for their afternoon naps. When she walked into their room, Harriet almost fainted. Bonnie had decided to do Ricky's nails with blood red fingernail polish. She had painted him up to his fat little elbows and poured the rest over the top of his strawberry blond head. "Of course, I thought he was bleeding," recalled Harriet, "and it scared me to death."

"Mother Dear," Harriet had wailed. "Come get Bonnie."

And how did her poor darling mother cope with Harriet's rambunctious, mischievous child?

Quite well. Bonnie was an angel at her house.

"Don't you DARE tell my children what I did!" pleaded Larry, the father of two preteens and one teenager. "I don't want to give them ideas."

His mother agreed. Heaven knows, she didn't want her grandchildren's mother to go through what she had. Her son wanted to go, go, go all the time. But the way he did it was often inappropriate.

* At age 9, Larry cranked up the family car, a Rambler station wagon, without a key and rode 'round and 'round in a field. Mama looked out the window and saw not only her own son in that bumping, thumping Rambler but the heads of his two

little cousins, ages 8 and 3, bobbing inside.

* At 10, he decided he didn't want to stay at his grandmother's one day, so he hid in the trunk of Mama's car. Many miles later, when she got out in front of the beauty salon where she worked, his mother heard a recognizable voice, "Mama, mama, I'm here, too."

* At 12, he was no longer satisfied riding his minibike around their property. He took it out on the highway, where only licensed drivers were supposed to travel. A policeman followed him home.

* At 13, he was home from school one morning when he got to wrestling with two neighborhood boys, who were three years older. The other two were definitely playing hooky. (There's still some question as to how sick Larry had been that day.) At any rate, in the tussle, one of the older boys broke her son's tooth with a ring. For Mama, this meant a very costly dental bill. But Larry got even: shot his buddy's tire out, so he couldn't go, go, go.

* At 14, he wanted a particular red Chevrolet so badly, he would do anything to get it. His best friend Billy showed him how he could pay for it. Billy copied Larry's father's name, and both of them took off for the bank.

"My daddy wrote this check so I can buy a car," Larry told the teller, handing over a $500 check.

A few minutes later, his father came storming into the bank.

* At 15, Larry still had no driver's license and no car, but that didn't stop him from taking his girlfriend 100 miles away to visit his paternal grandparents. When Mama missed the car, she notified the police. Not only had he taken the car, he had her credit cards and money! His parents found out where he was that night and went there the next day to pick him up.

Meanwhile, Larry somehow thought they wouldn't recognize the vehicle if it were a different color. So he took it to a graveyard and spray-painted Mama's gray Impala and its vinyl top a tacky gold. Never thought to change the license plate.

* At 16, he finally had a car of his own. Showing off, he got a speeding ticket. Where? Right in front of his house!

* At 18, he pulled another shocker for Mama. This time he drove across the state line with his 17-year-old girlfriend and married her.

Funny thing though. Larry straightened up real fast. He had to go to school, get a job and live with his parents.

No more wild rides.

CRIME & PUNISHMENT - KID STYLE

So who has never been more naughty than nice? Put yourself in *their* shoes.

Not long after being punished for bed-jumping, Benjamin was saying his prayers with his mother and older brother present. "God bless Mama and Daddy and Tyler. And God bless me because I'm going to jump on the bed as soon as Mama's out of the room."

Brent's mother is a housewife; his dad owns a construction company. Brent was quite young but talking well, when his mother punished him for disobedience, sending him to his room and bed.

Checking on him later, she said, "Well, Brent, I hope you know now that when Mommy tells you to do something you must do it."

"Are you my boss?" he asked.

"Yes, I guess you could say that."

Brent thought a moment, head cocked. "Mommy, is Daddy a woman?"

While shopping with his mom in a Seattle supermarket, 4-year-old William opened his mouth and bit what was in front of him. A banana? Bar of candy? Nope. His mother's buttock! Wow, was she mad! In front of all those customers, she bit him back. Bruised his...arm?

At the end of the school year, an evaluation was done to decide whether Tristan would continue in a learning disabled class or could be mainstreamed into a normal kindergarten.

One test was a series of questions to determine his social skills. The tester asked, "What do you say to people when you are in their home and you accidently break something that

66

belongs to them?"

Tristan looked at his mother, Monica, and his older brother, Austin. Then he turned to his teacher and, in his clearest voice, said, "I say 'Austin did it!'"

Sandra had told her boys, Michael and Pat to get into the car. She was fumbling at the back door, when it slammed shut. Her keys were inside. She closed her eyes. "Oh damn!" she said vehemently.

"Mama!" said a shocked Pat, age 5.

Michael's face brightened. "That means you've got to wash YOUR mouth out with soap!" said the delighted 7-year-old.

Rules are rules. Fair is fair. Justice, justice. Oh, drat!

After Danielle, 4, had been "grounded" for her misdeeds, she called her grandmother in Chesterfield, Missouri. "The next time Mommy does something wrong, will you ground her?"

Karen heard her son talking in his crib. When she went in to get him, he was repeating something she had told him earlier— "Do not write on Mommy's wall"—while scribbling on the wall with an ink pen.

Repeatedly—four, five or six times—little Chris had come home from school late and wet. His baby sitter, Joan, and Nan, his mother, had both punished him. Nan had talked with him each time, forbidding him to ever go to the neighborhood creek. But Chris never admitted playing in the creek. He'd only say that he had *fallen* in.

After another wet-clothes episode, Nan increased the punishment. She confined him to his room through the dinner hour until bedtime. Nan went in when he was ready for bed to hear him say his prayers.

"Dear God," said Chris. "Please don't let my feet fall off the stones."

My daughter Joy was being unusually naughty the night before Easter. "If you do that again," I threatened, "the Easter Bunny will bring you sticks and stones."

She did it.

Now what? I never dreamed she'd do it! She apparently never believed the Easter Bunny could be mean. And what would I do with the plastic eggs already filled with jelly beans and toys?

Joy put out her Easter basket in the usual spot in the den. (Her cheapskate mom had figured out some time ago that new baskets every year get expensive.) My husband Randy was no help. I was on my own. Do I not follow through on promised punishment just this once? When she was younger, I'd learned the hard way that undelivered punishment was an invitation to more undesirable behavior. And so I reluctantly went outside to hunt for twigs and gravel to put into the basket.

Of course, when the poor child saw her mournful basket the next morning, she burst into tears.

After a brief admonition, I suggested that perhaps the Easter Bunny had hidden the eggs around the house this year. Sure enough, there was one behind a curtain.

Joy was joyful again. Not only that, she wanted the Bunny to do that *every* year.

Sometimes, a parent isn't the only one to punish.

In an intense sibling rivalry involving four boys, Alex, the youngest, usually got the short end of every stick. A mere five years younger than his oldest brother, he eventually learned how to hold his own. He would bait them to the point of retaliation then tattle at just the right moment so that the three "thugs," as he affectionately calls them, got in trouble with Mom.

His brothers finally got back at him one day, though, when they discovered a headline in the *Atlanta Journal/Constitution* that stated "Every fourth child born in the world is Chinese." Barely old enough to read, Alex understood. He was obviously the fourth child. That shut him up for quite awhile, for he'd been convinced he wasn't even a part of the family.

Sandy's 4-year-old Emily was excited about attending her first professional basketball game. Initially, she was consumed by watching Charlotte's team mascot, Hugo the Hornet, and eating her cotton candy. But when the announcer called, "Time out, Hornets," Emily got a frantic look on her face. "Mommy, what did they *do* to have to go to time out?"

BIRDS & BEES & ADULT TREES

A foster mother I once knew gave up her charges when they reached puberty so that she wouldn't have to explain the birds and the bees. Real mothers can't do that. They only wish...

When their children were 10 and 11, Alice and Lucas decided it was time to explain the facts of life. Well-rehearsed, Alice took their daughter, Lisa, into one room and Lucas talked with son Bucky in another. Lesson over, they compared notes.

Lisa had been indignant. "I'm never going to do *that!*"

Bucky was aghast. "You mean you did that *twice*?"

At about age 10, Richie came in telling his mother some things he'd heard about sex. He asked her to tell him more. "I think you ought to talk with your Daddy," Annelle said.

A little while later, Richie returned. "*You'd* better tell me. He doesn't know any more than I do. He said, 'Tell me what you already know.'"

Big sister Claire was explaining the facts of life to her younger brother, Stuart. She had just told him that he used to be "in Mommy's tummy."

Stuart burst into noisy tears.

Their mother, Martha, came running from the other room. "What's wrong, Sweetie?"

He wailed, "Mommy would never eat Stuart all up!"

Musings and misconceptions:

While playing dolls, Katy looked up and asked, "Do you think I'll ever get married?"

"That's up to you, Katy."

"Will I marry a boy?"

"I hope so."

She smoothed out her doll's hair. "Gee, I wonder what I'll name him."

Adrienne's son, Jackie, age 6, had it all figured out why she had only two children: "You only have two breasts."

Mama overheard this conversation between her daughter Kate, 5, and Will, the 6-year-old son of friends:
"Will you marry me, Will?"
"Sure," said Will. "But don't we have to date first?"
"Naw, I want to go on the honeymoon right now."

Tony, 6, was listening when his mother, Debbie, and grandmother, Farrell, were talking about getting their dog spayed. He asked Debbie what that meant.
"It's getting fixed, so she can't have puppies," Debbie explained.
"Mom," he said, after a quiet moment, "I don't want any children for a while, so when I get married, I am going to get my wife spayed."

Annette's 3-year-old Michelle was taking her Uncle Barry on a tour of their home.
Pointing to a picture of Annette and her husband "pre-children," Barry asked, "Do you know who they are?"
Michelle smugly replied, "That's my Mommy and Daddy before I was a twinkle in their eyes."

His parents had paid a bundle to get a realistic Santa Claus to stop by their house to see Ben. They were videoing the momentous occasion.
Ben offered to show Santa his room. Up the elegant stairway they went, hand-in-hand.
"Who's that pretty lady in the wedding gown?" Santa asked, pointing to an oil painting on the landing.
"That's my mommy," said Ben, grinning for the video. "I'm in her tummy."
"No he's not!" snapped Mommy to the microphone. "He was born years later. I have the papers to prove it."

Anna's daughter, Denise, age 9, was filling out a form for her first magazine subscription. Proudly, she handed it over for the inspection. In the space marked "sex," she had carefully printed: "Haven't had it yet."

Judi and her son, David, were looking through a magazine hunting pictures for a first-grade homework assignment. They happened upon a photo featuring a man clowning around, pretending to kiss the hand of a half-naked statue of a woman.

"Oh yuck!" said David. "I would never kiss a girl with her clothes off!"

Okay, how would YOU answer these questions?

Benjamin, 4, had been rehearsing his Christmas play at school. His mommy, Nan, had also read the nativity story to him and his younger twin brothers at home. So, before bedtime, he asked, "If baby Jesus was born in a manger, why were my babies born in a hospital?"

'Splain that one, Mommy!

The kid grinned while the bride and groom were kissing. People in nearby pews heard him ask his mama in a loud whisper, "Has he sprinkled the pollen on her yet?"

"Gramma, do you still have sex?" asked Teddy at 5.

Mae, trying to assume the straightforwardness of the '90s, replied in as normal a tone as she could muster, "Yes."

"Do you do it with your clothes off?"

"I can't remember."

The "A" word, etc.

Martha, now in her 70s, told about studying the Ten Commandments for Sunday school. She was practicing her memory work at the kitchen table while her mother was washing dishes. Martha got to the seventh and realized she didn't know what it meant. "What's adultery?" she asked her mom.

Mother's elbows stiffened in the sink. A quick thinker, she

declared calmly, "Why Martha, that's when you stick out your tongue at your neighbor."

Martha clapped her hand over her mouth. Oh no! she thought. I've done that with my *brothers!*

Every time she saw someone poke a tongue out, she shook her head, knowing that they were committing sin number seven.

"I was 20 years old," she exclaimed, "before I found out my mama lied to me!"

John was a P.K. (preacher's kid, Methodist variety, 1940's version). At 5, he and some friends thought it would be fun to construct a pretend horror house, like the one they had seen at the fair. When he asked his saintly mother for some materials to do so, he was promptly spanked and sent to bed.

His simple request? "Could I have some sheets and blankets to build a hor' house?"

Decades later, a little boy was reciting the Ten Commandments. His mother stopped him at the seventh. "Do you know what this commandment is?" she asked.

"Sure," he replied proudly. "Don't cut adult trees."

SOMEBODY CONTROL THIS CHILD!

The scene is a family gathering, a public place—or worse—a major occasion. Your kid is on display, and he's acting up or talking out of turn.

When an older uncle died, the family gathered in his home the night before the funeral. The minister who was going to perform the service was there. He suggested that they go around the room so that each of the many relatives could tell what Tom had meant to him or her. Of course, he was seeking material for the eulogy.

After almost everyone had spoken, 5-year-old Matt raised his hand. His mother was pleased that he wanted to contribute.

"Matt, I'm sorry," said the preacher. "Do you want to tell what you remember about Uncle Tom?"

"Yes," said Matt. "We used to talk about farting."

"When you have three kids, it's really hard to synchronize bladders on a trip," said a North Carolina mother.

"We were coming home from Washington, D.C. one Sunday morning and our son kept saying, 'I have to pee-pee.'"

The mother, Robbye, kept assuring him that when they stopped for lunch—in just a minute—he could go. He kept whining, and she repeated, "As soon as you get out, you can pee."

Well, they pulled up in front of the Daniel Boone restaurant near Durham, and he took her literally—ran to the nearest bush and did his thing behind it.

Only trouble was that, on the other side of the bush, was a plate glass window. Inside sat several senior citizens trying to eat their Sunday dinner while he whizzed at them.

Nan took her twin sons, Justin and Vincent, to the library to get some Charlie Brown videotapes. When the librarian told them there were no more available, Justin got very cross and exploded, "Lady, you're fired!"

73

"Martha!" exclaimed a neighbor who had phoned. "I'm so sorry to hear that you and Wayne are getting a separation!"

"Well, I can't imagine how you heard," Martha said unhappily. "Wayne and I haven't told a soul."

"Oh," said the neighbor. "Your son Tommy is standing in the front yard, telling everyone passing by."

Rita was ready to throw in the towel at the end of an afternoon at a suburban swimming pool in University Heights, Ohio. Worn out as a mother of five, Rita watched grimly as her two youngest sons, Jim, a curly blond of 3, and his dark-haired brother Rick, 4, began to fight. She had them with her in the women's shower room, where their shouts and punches resounded.

Abruptly, a woman strode over to them. "If you don't stop," she warned loudly. "I'm going to tell your mothers!"

The American family had not been living in Italy very long when they went sightseeing. Little David was intrigued by a fountain of a cherub peeing a gentle arc of water. Amid a bevy of tourists, David imitated the cherub.

Just take 'em shopping and see what happens.

Friends and neighbors chuckled over Bobby's nickname for his father. Just learning to talk, Bobby loved the attention he got whenever he used it. But father John wasn't amused when he took his son grocery shopping. All the shoppers and clerks in the store were, though, for the little fellow trailed his daddy up one aisle and down the next calling, "Mama, Mama!"

Dana, who was not yet 3, couldn't say the consonant blend "tr." It always came out "ff."

Family members thought that was cute until her Aunt Linda took her to a store one day and Dana spied a truck she wanted. She pointed and loudly demanded the "F" word. Customers turned around wide-eyed, as she repeated it over and over.

Linda promised to buy it if she wouldn't say it again. Later Linda recalled, "I bought that truck and got outta there."

Wheeling their cart toward the food store exit, Brett, a preschooler, asked loudly, "Mom, what did you steal *this* time?"

Thoroughly mortified, Maria sputtered that she'd never stolen as much as a grape from this or any other store.

"Yes you did steal something. You do it every time we're here," he said with enough emphasis to cause heads to turn. Then he lowered his voice. "You got five packets of drink mix, and she only put one over that beeping thing. You stole four of them."

Standing in a grocery store check-out lane, Abbie's son, Hunter, 4, pulled at her. "Mommy, look! That lady walks funny!"

True, the grossly obese woman was waddling, as she pushed her cart ahead of them.

Abbie was frowning and trying to shush her child, when suddenly a ham dropped from between the huge woman's legs.

"Mommy!" cried Hunter. "She's had a baby!"

The fat lady whirled, glared and indignantly demanded, "Who threw that at me? Who did that?"

"She's had a baay-bee!" Hunter howled.

"Somebody threw that!" The shopper stared at Hunter and then stormed out of the store, leaving the cart in the line, ham on the floor.

No one. No one would touch that ham.

"There I was, so upset that my son would embarrass that woman," recalled Abbie, "and *she* lays a ham!"

Why is it that so many embarrassing incidents occur at church?

Diane's five-year-old Margaret joined the throng at the staid Episcopal church, as they solemnly filed past the living tableaux of the nativity scene. The mother was aghast, however, when her daughter stopped on the chancel steps, put both hands on her hips and said with loud disgust, "That's not Baby Jesus! That's Baby Tender Love!"

The church was filled to capacity on Easter Sunday. While the children were gathered around for a children's sermon, the minister turned to a 7-year-old. "Ellen, that's a mighty pretty dress you have on."

In a voice that carried all the way to the back pews, she declared, "Yeah, but my mama says it's a bitch to iron."

Betty was proud of her Kim, age 4, who, along with other little girls were showing off the memory verses they could say. The text that Kim supposedly had learned was, "If you want to live long in the land that God has given you, honor your mother and father."

But the verse that Kim said in front of the congregation was "If you want to live, honor your mother."

One Sunday, Lisa's family was attending a communion service at church. Her 4-year-old son watched with interest as the bread and then the wine was passed out among the parishioners. When the sacrament was completed, he leaned over to Lisa to say in a very loud whisper, "It was a very small picnic, wasn't it?"

Little Margo, age 4, was sitting quietly during the sermon in a very large Episcopal sanctuary when she decided to play with the toy she had hidden under her coat. Before her mother could stop her, she had pulled the peanut out of the elephant's mouth the full extension of the cord. "Around the World in 80 Days" blared forth. The minister spoke not a word until the whole song had played.

Kathye sometimes worried about Sam having the middle-child syndrome with its accompanying low self-esteem—that is, until his nursery school class was gathered in their Pennsylvania church while the minister was explaining the greatness and awesomeness of God. "Who among us..?" he marveled. "Who among us can say we are perfect?"

Sam's hand shot up. "I'm perfect."

Late to church that Sunday night, the young family had to sit on the front row.

"Our preacher is one to give good eye contact," said Michael's mother, "and we felt he was preaching right to us."

Michael, age 3, was behaving well during the sermon until

he looked to the right and gave a loud sniff. Then he sniffed to the left. "Mama! Somebody pooted!"

The preacher began "uh, uh, uhing," as he flipped pages to find his place.

"And I wanted to crawl into the hymnal," recalled Mama.

The family had been church-shopping until they visited one they really liked. As the collection plate passed in front of their 4-year-old daughter, she dropped in some Monopoly money. Embarrassed, her mother Juanita reached in and plucked it out.

In a shrill voice that only a child can muster, the daughter shrieked, *"Don't you take God's money!"*

Mom dropped it like sizzling bacon.

And no one in that family ever set foot in that church again.

Susan and her husband were teaching first grade Sunday school at their affluent Baptist church. For several weeks they had been studying the prophets.

Before moving on to Jeremiah, Susan asked the children if they could recall what a prophet was.

Their daughter Rachel was the only one to raise her hand. As she bobbed up and down waiting to be called on, Susan beamed. "My angel has listened and even remembered!" she thought happily.

Susan asked Rachel to tell the class, and the child stood proudly to announce, "A prophet is when you make more money than you spend."

Watch them at weddings!

Flower girls, usually preschoolers, are unpredictable. For instance, while front and center:

* One loudly sang "Old MacDonald Had a Farm."
* Another performed her favorite dance, the hula.
* Still another stuck her fingers in her ears the whole time her aunt, the soloist, was singing.
* Warned not to move, a tyke wet the floor at her feet.
* A Chattanooga flower girl jealously demanded to hold the pillow. The ring bearer guarded it with his life. A noisy tug-

of-war ensued.

 * Dying to see what was under the bride's antebellum dress, a little cutie tilted the hoop. She saw. So did everyone else.

 * She looked distressed before the throw-up. Then she splattered the whole front row.

Her mother, the matron of honor, didn't notice at first, but the front three rows in the church were crying, trying to stifle out-loud giggles. The 2-year-old flower girl had gotten hot. She was shedding clothes like a writhing snake. Had to drop to the floor to do it, what with the thumb in the mouth. The tights were down over the shoes; the slip covered her curls.

The preacher had just glanced over the heads of the kneeling bride and groom and was having a bit of trouble getting out the words of his prayer. That's when the kid's mother peeked. She rushed to get her child up off the floor. Now we all know how a toddler can protest, so with the first yelp, the embarrassed mother did the only thing she could think of: stretched her skirt, curtsy-style, to screen the scene. Too late.

Now what would YOU have done? Your 7-year-old son, a ring bearer, was twitching around and misbehaving in the front of the sanctuary during a wedding in a prestigious church. Would you have ignored him? This child's mother called him down.

With that, he told her in no uncertain terms where she could go, threw the little satin pillow at her and flipped the bird at the entire congregation.

Seated in the congregation at a relative's wedding, the mother of the 4-year-old ring bearer was stunned by her son's behavior.

Standing nice-as-you-please in his little white tuxedo, he was making horrible sounds. "Grrrrrr! Rowllll! Rrrrrrrroar!"

She put her finger to her lips. Then she waved her arms to get his attention.

He would not look at her. He did not shut up. The poor minister just had to raise his voice and go on.

Finally, when it was all over, the mother pulled her child aside. "Son, why were you making all those strange noises?"

"I was just bein' what I 'sposed to be," he explained innocently, "a ring bear."

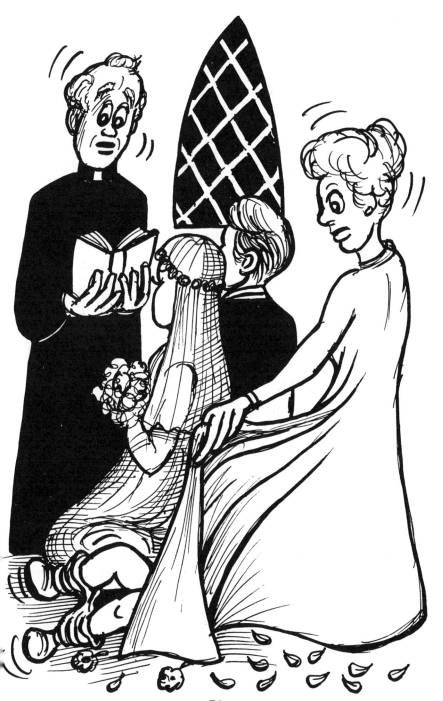

TEENS—TOO TRYING FOR WORDS

If you thought the "terrible twos" were tough, you'll be wishing you could return to those blissful years, when your kids turn teen. At least, in earlier days, you had some degree of control and credibility.

Why was having a teenager such a shock? I think I have a clue: my own teen years.

Now I was far from perfect back then, but it never crossed my mind that rules were made to be broken.

"Yeah, right," you say in a tone of disbelief.

Yeah, right. In fact, in those dark ages, "teen years" ended at 21.

And so, on the morning of my 21st birthday, I did not pick up the nasty concoction above my plate. For nearly two years, I had been required to drink vinegar and honey before every breakfast I ate at home. "Because it's good for what ails you," Daddy would say.

I used to wish I'd barf into my eggs just once to show my parents how nauseous I felt.

"Drink your vinegar and honey *before* you eat," Mother reminded me.

I politely reminded *her* that I was now 21, and I was not going to ever drink it again.

Mother cried. I had "defied" her!

One curious thing, though. After that morning, neither Mother nor Daddy ever drank that stuff again.

Billy had been difficult to raise throughout his teen years. Among other things, he had hung around with the wrong crowd, stolen a car and gotten kicked out of military school. His relationship with Mom remained strained for years until THE CALL.

Billy was blubbering so that she could hardly understand him between sobs, but what he said endeared him to her the rest of her life. "I'm so sorry...so sorry...I gave you such a hard time...when I was a teenager," he wailed. "I know what you went through...(sniff)...now that I have...three!"

"Is tonight the night you have your nervous breakdown?" asked Enid's teenage son, Brad.

She always had what he called a "breakdown" the night before a family vacation. Preparing and packing for four kids and a husband to spend a week at a vacation place got her down. That afternoon was typical. Brad had brought his team home, and they drank 18 cans of soft drinks and ate who-knows-how-much of the snack food she'd just bought for the trip.

Kathy's teenage son Michael had a problem: whenever he tried anything, he always got caught. (Other kids should be so lucky!)

Kathy gave a prime example:

She and her husband, Bruce, were driving past a convenience store in their neighborhood and spotted Michael's car in the parking lot. "Oh, I hope he's not in there buying junk food," she had said.

Bruce shook his head. "Not junk food." He pulled into the lot.

As Michael and three buddies were returning to their car with a 12-pack of beer, Kathy and Bruce jumped out and with false grins hollered, "Beer patrol!"

Son Michael grumbled at his back luck. His friends groaned. "Are you going to call our parents?"

"No," said Bruce calmly. "You are."

Said Bet's teenage son to his mother with vehemence: "I am NOT arguing!"

Remembering the difficult year when their rebellious teenager, Judy (one of three girls), ran away from home, Ethel confessed, "We called a family conference to decide whether we wanted her back."

"We've heard that it's better for mothers and their teenagers if they don't talk except about mundane things," said a father. "Everything goes fine with my wife and daughter when they're saying, 'Turn here' or 'Dinner's ready.'"

"Really?" I said. "How old is your daughter?"

"Eight."

Just who embarrasses whom? Hmmm?

Bevie's son, Bill, was among the 8th graders who moved up to the high school where she was teaching. That first day, while walking down a crowded hall, she discovered that her name had changed from "Mom" to a snarled, "Keep moving!"

"Why is it," asks Cathy, "that your kids beg and beg you to go to their games, and you go and sit in the bleachers—and then you're not allowed to even wave?"

Donna's just-turned-teen Toby had a habit of forgetting to tell her his after-school plans: where he was going, how he was getting home, when to expect him, all the details he could communicate with a simple phone call.

Exasperated, Donna threatened, "If you don't call me right away, I shall come to wherever you are and embarrass you mercilessly in front of your friends.

Toby gasped. "You already do!"

Sometimes a mother's instructions are taken too literally.

A piano teacher in Norfolk, Virginia, Ginny's mother had taught her daughters not to disturb her during a lesson. Ginny recalls the afternoon her older sister somehow cut Ginny's arm with a scythe. Blood. Slashed skin. More blood.

Sis grabbed Mother's keys from her purse and raced Ginny across a busy bridge to the hospital several miles away. From the emergency room, she called their dad.

"How did you get there?" he asked.

"I drove," replied the 15-year-old, who had never before taken the car out of the driveway.

Those early driving years drive parents nuts.

Anita was reluctant to let her daughter borrow the car because it was the only one the family owned. Generally, Babs was a responsible child, but she had just gotten her license. So Anita set some limits.

Babs could drive her best friend, a neighbor (but no one

else) to the Sunday night youth meeting at church (but nowhere else) and must be home before dark (it was daylight savings time).

As the best friend, I can attest that she drove carefully to the church. But her boyfriend, Dan, wasn't there. In fact, Dan had been seen with a girl named Ann at school that week. As we were turning toward home, Babs thought aloud, "I bet I know where Dan is."

With that, she headed in the opposite direction. I knew we were both in trouble when she entered another neighborhood far from home.

Sure enough, there was Dan's car. And there was Dan, seated on a sofa in front of a picture window, his arm around Ann. "Doesn't bother me a bit," she said haughtily, as she drove completely up a guy wire on the telephone pole across the street.

The front tires were still spinning as we jumped down from our perch. Dan and Ann came running out to see what idiot had hit the pole. "Babs! What are *you* doing here?" he said. Ann ran back to her house.

Babs was too hysterical and too scared to call her parents. Her dad would be furious; her mom, devastated. That was the family's only car. Besides, someone else would have to drive us home, because only a wrecker could take that car anywhere.

I reluctantly called my father to explain the predicament and ask him to come. Then *I* became the furious one. Daddy was laughing himself silly.

Elizabeth's driving record was an embarrassment to both her parents. As she was leaving to return to college, her father sternly warned her not to get another speeding ticket. A few hours later, the phone rang, and her mother answered. "Elizabeth wants to talk to you," she said, calling to her husband in another room.

Thomas was seething as soon as he heard her say, "I got stopped by the highway patrol."

She quickly added, "Dad, the patrolman found some marijuana in the back seat."

His demeanor switched from anger to horror. "No, Elizabeth, no!" Horrible thoughts brought sobs. Where had he gone wrong? How long had this been going on? Was she addicted? What would his fellow state legislators, or his constituents, think? He had advocated getting tough on drugs. How could he deal with her—or them?

He was still emotional, when she said, "Just kidding, Dad. I only got a speeding ticket."

His relief was evident. "Is that all? Are you sure? Don't worry, I'll get a lawyer to help you."

He wasn't even mad at Elizabeth's mother, Jane, who had quickly suggested the ploy to show him how all things are relevant.

At 16, Elise had just gotten her driver's license. When she asked to borrow her mother's car to take a friend to the library one afternoon, Mom was unperturbed. Elise was a responsible child and quite studious.

But Mom got really upset when Elise didn't come home for dinner. Hours ticked by. About 9 p.m., the phone rang. Mom sensed real trouble when Elise asked to speak to Dad. But she'd just had a flat tire.

Dad got on the phone. "Sure, Elise, I'll come get you. Where are you? WHERE?"

Their daughter was beside the highway near Boone in the mountains of North Carolina, about 100 miles from home.

"The Charlotte library didn't have what we needed," she explained. "So we went to the one at Appalachian State."

Late one night, the phone awakened Mary Ellen. A policeman identified himself and asked, "Do you have a son named Paul?"

"Yes."

"Do have a Buick?"

"Yes."

"Do you know where it is?"

"In my garage."

"You'd better go look."

Mary Ellen peered out the window. The car was gone. She returned to the phone. "It's not there!"

"It's here," said the smug policeman. "And Paul is at police court with his buddies."

"Well you tell Paul that it's entirely too late for him to be out," huffed Mary Ellen. "And he must come home immediately!"

Nice try Mom. It didn't work.

It's a time of pets/pests and parties.

"If you want to eat here, no snakes" had been the rule of the house set forth by the mother of three teenagers (two boys). The youngest, Walt, whom Lyn describes as a "pet freak," had brought home animals of all descriptions. One day he dared bring in a grey rat snake. In a weak moment, she agreed that, if it stayed in his old aquarium with a roof taped on in the basement, she would tolerate it. She didn't realize that that meant a mouse cage, too, and then a mouse-breeding operation to provide food for this most loathed of pets. As the snake grew, so did the size of mice.

Soon after they returned from a brief vacation, someone noticed that the limbless reptile was not in his habitat. Sometimes, it would hibernate under the dirt, but not this time. It was gone. Lyn immediately phoned the local nature museum.

"We get a lot of calls from mothers of teenagers," the spokesman said. "You're worried about whether he'll get in bed with you."

Yes, indeed she was. He assured Lyn that their pet would come up the basement steps only if he wanted out. Snakes prefer warmth and moisture, he said, and theirs would probably be happy in the basement.

Lyn had been away from home for a few days and, upon her return, took some laundry down to the washing machine. Opening the top, she saw her son's dirty clothes already inside and something else that looked suspiciously like a snake.

She called its owner downstairs. Promptly.

Walt came and investigated. Muttering something about a shoestring, he derided her for being so squeamish.

Two weeks later, she opened the top and saw what she was certain was that cussed thing. Again, Walt—and even her husband—assured her that it was her imagination. Only clothes were in there. Walt worried aloud about her being under a great deal of strain coupled with advancement of age.

Hubby, Joe, did turn the machine upside down and examine it for any hole big enough for a snake to slither through. There was none.

The next incident, three weeks later, was even more frightening. There it was, curled around the inside rim of the machine. She carefully closed the top and ran for Joe. Yes, he saw it. He believed! He tried to grab it near the head, but the elusive one hustled to get back between the tub and the outer wall of the machine, and Joe could only catch it near the tail. It stiffen-

ed and wedged itself into an irretrievable position.

Lyn got some long scissors, but neither she nor Joe could use them. Theirs was a "politically correct" household, and violence was out of the question.

Bleach! Worth a try. While Joe held the body part as best he could with two hands, Lyn reached around both sides of her protector and held an open bottle of bleach near their captive. After a couple of whiffs, it relaxed, and Joe easily removed it from the hiding place.

Did he sling it out the basement door? Take it to some far-off woods? Nope. While Lyn was falling apart, Joe was petting it. Eventually, he put it back into the aquarium.

Walt, however, traded it for an iguana.

Sue found her teenage son's note in the kitchen. "There's a creature in my bathroom," it said. "It's big! Please get it out while I'm gone. Bring a gun."

The door to his bathroom was closed.

A gun, huh? B-B or bazooka? Sue cracked the door, eye-sized. The creature was in the line of sight: a luna moth was on the mirror.

Amy, her friends and their mothers were planning an upcoming spring break beach trip. After determining rules and curfews, they turned their attention to meals. Mothers volunteered to bring snacks like hot dogs and hamburgers.

That was when Amy asked, "Who's going to bring the condoms?"

Mary and her husband Joe arrived home after an overnight summer visit and were relieved to find the house still standing. Despite their admonitions to their two teenagers not to have any parties, they wondered if the temptation of no chaperones would be too great.

They checked the house carefully. It had been freshly vacuumed. Mary peered into the garbage. No beer cans. Later, Joe was walking in the backyard and spied the remains of a block of ice. He smugly called John, his oldest, for an explanation. He and Mary awaited the answer.

Without blinking, John retorted, "We had the biggest freak hailstorm you ever saw last night."

And learning to become a consumer:

Colleen called her mom soon after she arrived at Vanderbilt University. The sophisticated teenager was pleased to report to Linda that she and her roommate, Laura, had heeded their parents' warning about watching their funds. Rather than stocking up on snack foods from the convenience store on campus, they had called a cab to take them to a supermarket. They shopped there for bargains while the driver waited outside with the meter running.

Mildred's cute blond daughter Joanie resented the "dumb blond" jokes popular during her freshman year in college. Mildred, who is *not* blond, wondered if the jokesters were on to something when Joanie declared that the constant increase in gasoline prices didn't affect *her*. "I never buy but $10 worth," she said.

A short time later, Joanie defied her critics by becoming an instant brunette.

Truer words were never typed.

While trying to collect stories for this chapter, I went online into AOL chat rooms. Usually, I chose one labeled "Over Forty."

"Hi! I'm working on my next humor book," I'd type. "It's about mothers. Anybody here a mom?"

Of the 22 others in the room, generally six or seven would reply. "I am," "me," or another such indication. At least one more would ask, "Do grandmas count?"

Then I'd soon be typing, "Got any funny stories as the mother of a teenager?"

Invariably, every time I tried this, some wise gal would type in caps (which is shouting), "THERE'S NOTHING FUNNY ABOUT BEING THE MOTHER OF A TEENAGER!"

MOTHER EMBARRASSES HERSELF, NO HELP FROM THE KIDS

In the role of being a mother, some women run into foot-in-mouth trouble—or worse. It can start really early.

Corinne, a wedding guest on the back pew was trying to be as unobtrusive as possible with her 18-month-old baby on her lap. When the procession started, she moved over so that her child could see. Her purse dropped noisily to the floor, and a pound-and-a-half of jelly beans rolled down the aisle.

At a church baptism, the congregation was agog when the infant's parents were presenting him to the preacher. Somehow, something flipped out of mother Delia's dress and flopped on the floor. Her falsies.

Jill had been trying to teach Todd not to stand in the middle of the floor and scream for her. But she heard him all the way from the basement howling, "Mom! Mom!"

She didn't respond.

Three minutes later, he yelled again. "Mom! Mom!"

This time, she headed for the basement. There was Todd, who had tried to open a closet door. He was bent over double beneath the heavy door, which had fallen off the hinges.

Pudgy, the pet pig owned by a western Massachusetts family, had been roaming the front yard before he took off for parts unknown. Mom grabbed a bucket of Pudgy's favorite food to run after him. When he caught the scent of dinner, the 500-pound pet turned on its heels and began chasing Mom.

By the tenth time around the circular driveway, Mom was exhausted and frantic. But all the children were roaring with laughter. It was the kids who screamed prudent advice: "Drop the bucket!"

The bucket dropped. Pudgy stopped. Mom plopped.

Renee and her sons had worked really hard one evening to make the perfect snowman. Wishing Mr. Snowman good night, they retired happily. The next morning they were dismayed to see that Mr. Snowman had taken a nosedive onto the ground.

That explains why Renee found herself alone at 7 a.m. in Illinois's freezing December weather, her bare feet stuck in a pair of boots, nightgown hanging below her coat, hair sticking out of a ski cap diligently packing together a snowman. While pushing a big ball of snow around the yard, she was startled to see bewildered looks from neighbors as they drove by on their way to work. Renee just waved.

Violet, 35, had taken Dee, 8, to an American Girl doll club meeting at a local bookstore. After the speakers related true stories about World War II, Violet stepped up to them to chat. "I've been telling my children that World War I was with Germany and World War II with Japan. That's right, istn't it?"

Irene could smell Kaity's problem during the movie: number two in the panties. Embarrassed, she whisked her up and rushed to the restroom. Later, standing in the stall, Irene wondered what to do next. In her frustration, she had just flushed Kaity's new underwear down the toilet.

With three children, ages 1 to 5, in day care, Liz has been overwhelmed with art work on a daily basis. As a rule, some winds up on the refrigerator, but most ends up being acknowledged and secretly trashed.

One spring morning, Liz gathered up a cubby-full of her 3-year-old's paintings from the day care when she dropped her off. Then she hurried on to her job.

At lunchtime, she and a co-worker were headed for her car when they passed the mesh trash can in the parking lot. "Look at that!" said her friend. "Can you believe someone would actually trash their child's art. What a terrible parent!"

At Betty Carol's tenth birthday party, Mama was trying to cut the big birthday cake she had lovingly baked. The knife got tangled, as the large gathering of children watched. Tangled in what? Something baked into the batter. A kitchen dish rag.

Moms can't escape embarrassment, even out of town.

Back in the '30s, on a family trip from Baltimore to New York, little Harriet made a deposit in her white enamel potty. Her mother quickly got rid of the odorous contents: she dumped it in a paper bag and threw it out the window.

A horn began to blow behind them.

"What's the matter with that nut?" said Dad. "Where does he expect me to go? He can't pass me on this bridge!"

Mom turned around to see a rather brown windshield. Dad glanced in the rear view mirror, turned white and stomped the gas pedal. So did the man behind him.

Both of them bounced off the bridge and tore up the road. Mom begged Dad to stop. Dad, fearing broken bones, finally complied. Mom and Dad walked contritely toward the windshield smeared brown from end to end.

An apology and good cleaning job later, the other driver chuckled, "I thought World War II had started and they were using some new kind of bomb."

On her first outing as a Brownie leader, Jayne led the girls on a nature hike, where they found a little pond teeming with tadpoles. She encouraged them to collect some in jars while they were playing in the water. Jayne thought it was a terrific experience for those urban kids—until they returned to their meeting room, got out a magnifying glass and made a startling discovery. Shrieking, the Brownies ran to dump the jars outside.

They left Jayne to explain to their mothers why the girls were so frantic: the "tadpoles" were actually mosquito larvae!

Brave Eleanor took her children camping in the wild. All night long, she complained of being cold, of "catching a chill." This is the mother who always made sure that her brood were all snug and warm. But Eleanor never figured out how to use a sleeping bag. She had slept under it instead of in it.

During a trip to Acapulco, Jan found some beautiful jewelry of gilded maple leaves, which she bought for her daughter. The youngster and her junior high friends thought it was "cool."

Only they weren't maple leaves. They were marijuana.

On a family vacation in South Carolina, Sue Beth and her husband took their three daughters to a water park near Myrtle Beach. Mitzi, the 5-year-old thought she could keep up with her big sisters, ages 7 and 9, until reaching the top of the stairs to the long twisty-twirly waterslide. "Mommy! Mommy!" she yelled.

Mommy to the rescue. Never having regained her slim figure after pregnancy, Sue Beth truly struggled to push her way up the steps getting to her frightened baby. At the top, she calmed the child by assuring her that she would not go down alone.

Sue Beth had already ignored the sign "If you are taller that this, don't go on this ride." But she figured that dragging her little one down the steps where no other child would budge from his place in line would be worse than zipping speedily down the slide. She positioned Mitzi between her legs and let loose.

Whee! That first turn was a tilter. Sue Beth's left hip rose higher than the right, and she nearly lost any sense of balance. The second turn was the killer. Somehow she was folded, butt up, over her child, who was screaming again, and they were wedged tight in the colorful tube. With frantic heroic movements, she freed Mitzi's face from the swishing water, but both remained stuck in the tubing.

"Help me! Help me!" Mitzi yelled. Sue Beth tried to shush her with reassurances that Mama would wiggle them out soon.

Why doesn't my husband come help? Sue Beth wondered. Maybe he didn't recognize his daughter's voice. Maybe he didn't know where they were. But hubby was a member of a prominent Carolina family. Maybe he would be too embarrassed.

Someone called 911, and people were ordered out of the water ride area.

Fire truck sirens alerted everyone within hearing distance of their problem, and rescuers began a long series of maneuvers to free them. Would they have to take the tubing apart? Or cut it with a can-opener device? Good possibilities, but suddenly, with one fireman pushing her tailbone and others pulling her legs, first Mitzi and then Sue Beth came unstuck.

The crowd cheered and clapped until she splatted into the pool beneath the slide, whacked into two of her rescuers and knocked them down.

Her impulse was to stand and take a bow. But when Sue Beth pushed back her wet hair with her hands and opened her eyes, there stood her horrified in-laws. Hubby was stepping backwards.

While living overseas, Lydia went sightseeing with her children in India. At the Taj Mahal, she glanced across the reflecting pool to see her 18-month-old, Margaret, squatting to splash her hand in the water. Horrified, she strode across a crosswalk to save her child from sure drowning. Of course, *she* was the one to slip and fall into the pool. But it was a mere two feet deep, mostly algae.

Only her dignity was hurt, although bruised badly. Lydia grabbed her children and rushed to the car. Their driver, probably concerned more about his upholstery than her well-being, urged her to return to the motel and change.

"No, no," she said, trying to stay nonchalant. "Let's go on to the next place."

The young man drove them directly to their motel. "Madam," he said firmly. "Soon you will be stinky."

On a weekend trip to San Antonio, Carolyn took her two young children downtown for a riverboat cruise. Suddenly, it began to pour. Then hail. The threesome rushed into a nearby hotel to wait out the storm. But the precipitation didn't let up.

Finally, she bundled her brood into a taxi to get to her car (the location of which she had been careful to note).

After a five-minute taxi ride, the three arrived at the car. Once safely inside, Carolyn looked across the street. There stood the hotel she had just left.

Margaret was incredibly nervous about her seventh-grade son's first football game. She was convinced Donnie would suffer a bruising or worse. Nevertheless she would not miss his game.

Because it was an out-of-town game, she set out early. The stadium was a little hard to find, but she got there in time and found a place in the stands. She then spent the entire game on the edge of her seat, cheering for Number 12.

Finally the game ended, and Margaret ran to the sidelines to greet Donnie. Only then did she discover that the child wearing the 12 jersey was a total stranger and that she was at the wrong game, the wrong school and, uh, the wrong town.

PA system: "Will the mother who is lost please get found immediately by your son at Gate 5 with the Uzi?"

When a child marries, the limelight shines on Mom as well as the bride and groom.

To understand this not-quite-mother-of-the-groom, you need to know that Sue's a member of an organization that cares for wounded birds and other small creatures of the wild.

Two workmen next door had been cleaning out a chimney and threw some baby chimney swifts on the ground. Sue scooped them up and dished out some choice words at the culprits. She got her husband to build a false chimney (yes, out of real bricks) so that the birdies would have a familiar home. And then at frequent intervals, she fed them. To do this, Sue dampened a sticky mess of dehydrated bugs with spit, crept out a window onto the roof, over to the false chimney. She usually did the 6:30 a.m. feeding in her nightgown.

Enter her son's girlfriend-not-quite-fiancee from out of town. Allison spent the night in the guest room. The next morning at breakfast, she had a question for Sue. "I have to ask you something," she began slowly. "Early this morning, someone went through my bedroom, climbed out the window, stayed a few minutes and came back through. Was that you?"

She listened intently to the answer. And to Sue's surprise, Allison married her son anyway.

Brand new mother of the bride, now eating her words: "Horrible Harry is going to be my sweet wonderful son-in-law."

Being a mother of the bride is not easy until the ceremony itself. She may have had to take care of every detail beforehand, but at the ceremony, all she has to do is walk down that aisle, look pretty and sit in her seat.

One bride's mother was nervous anyway. She stopped off in the ladies room. When her turn came, all eyes were upon her. And she did look lovely, her pink chiffon gown just a flowin.' But, in her hand, she was clutching a roll of pink toilet paper. Her pink clutch purse was on the back of the commode.

While the stepmother of the bride headed down the aisle, a ripple of laughter began from the rear of the groom's side and followed her all the way to her seat. The back of her dress was tucked into the right side of her pantyhose.

Even when the child is grown and gone...

A 50-something mother and schoolteacher was appearing for jury duty. To plan for this civic obligation, Dot had had to find a substitute and make lesson plans for a week.

After answering all the judge's questions, she was waiting for other prospective jurors to be examined.

A young man was arguing with the judge because his card had been sent to his father's address. He was a "junior," and his father, the "senior," was too old to serve. The question was who had really been called, and the audience was laughing about his trying to wiggle out of serving.

That bothered Dot, for when the judge had read out her name, he had said Dorothy A. Elmore. She was Dorothy E. Elmore. She looked at her card. Sure enough, it had her daughter's name on it. Dorothy A. was a student at Duke University. Dot raised her hand. "That was my daughter's name you called out. Do you wish me to serve?"

The audience roared, particularly when she added the part about all the arrangements she had already made. But the judge released her anyway.

As Dot was walking out, the president of a local bank, an acquaintance, called out, "Don't you teach reading?"

YOU CAN'T OUTLAW MOTHERS-IN-LAW

Apparently there's not much funny about being a mother-in-law or having one. Here are all the stories I could collect.

Okay, I DID get a few:

What do you do when your mother-in-law hates her grandson-in-law? And you are taking her 1,000 miles to visit him, your only daughter and grandbaby. For Christmas.

The cause of her intense hatred is her own short-term memory loss. She does not remember that Mike thanked her for a very fine gift she gave him. He did, but every time we tried to repeat his exact words, she would say, "You lie! You're just trying to stand up for him!" When the poor boy tried to thank her again, that just made her madder. "Too little too late!" she snorted.

Before our trip, she announced that she was not going to give him a Christmas present. My husband tried to reason with her. "Mother, we are going to be a guest in his home. The least you can do is write a check to both of them."

"I will NOT!" she said with venom. "He's not getting any of MY money!"

That's when we got stomach cramps and insomnia. A couple of days before we were to leave, my husband was even saying he didn't want to go. Of course he did. He just couldn't think of a good reason to leave his mother behind. Try as I might, I couldn't either.

But something strange happened. The further we got from home, the more disoriented she became. When she was greeted at the airport by Mike, she was reasonably pleasant, although she was more focused on the baby. By Christmas Eve, we realized that her short-term memory had done *us* a favor: she had forgotten that she hated Mike.

Oh Christmas morning, she turned to her son. "I think I'll write them each a check," I heard her whisper. She pulled a check and a pen from her purse. "What's his name?"

A dignified woman, Bee had a quick sense of humor. However, those two facets of her personality never quite reconciled over the issue of comic strips. She saw nothing funny about them, period.

Bee kept a running argument on the subject with Tunk, her son-in-law. "They are absolutely childish!" she exclaimed in derision time and again.

However childish comic strips might be, Bee loved her son-in-law. She proved it for years—by mailing him the cartoon wrappers from her bubble gum.

Quite a few years ago, a newlywed, who had just come to this country from Ireland, was preparing to entertain her in-laws for dinner. Making a good impression on her new American mother-in-law was her prime goal. She bought chocolate candy for dessert. After the meal, she broke the squares evenly, placed them on a pretty plate and passed them around.

Her sister-in-law came rushing into the kitchen behind her. "You just served my parents Ex-Lax!"

Now, here's a rare mother-in-law.

"Did you hear that Farrah's daughter and son-in-law came to live with her?"

"Really?"

"Yes, and they brought six cats and three dogs."

"No kids?"

"No, but her daughter decided she didn't want to be married anymore, so she left."

"All of them?"

"Yes, but when I asked Farrah how things were going, she said, 'Fine. I *like* Ronald.'"

On being a mother-in-law:

"When I come home from my son's or daughter's home, I always have the sorest lip," said Mary, "from keeping my mouth zipped."

THERE'S NO SUCH THING
AS AN EMPTY NEST

You miss 'em desperately. For about three weeks. The first time. Then you and Dad get used to those uninterrupted private times together, a phone that has a dial tone whenever you want to use it and the freedom to travel on a whim.

And then they're back. First from camp, then college. Just any job or any apartment won't do. And meanwhile... "Rent? For my ole room?" You bet, but it's not high enough. "Rules? I'm not a kid anymore!" Traffic cops enforce rules on adults, why not parents?

Finally, one ventures back out into the real world—and then a sibling returns to sponge.

At last, they're all married or immersed in a job. But guess what? Now, it's a separation, divorce or layoff. Or a visit—with spouse and children and pets. Sooooo, why not? You might've gotten lonely.

Naaaaah!

A businessmom had a free couple of hours and invited her 28-year-old live-in son to meet her for lunch. Two of his friends stopped by their table at the restaurant.

"Did you guys ever get that third bedroom fixed up?" she asked.

"Yep," said one.

"How much rent would you charge?"

He told her.

She whirled toward her son, "I'll pay half!"

After eight years of being the puddle from which her grown son sponged, Ann was ready to get her own life.

First the excuse was school, then he was doing temp work. Lastly, he was bartending, making plenty of money, but this was not a "real job."

Ann thought surely she could force him to face his future and get on with it. She sold her four-bedroom house and took a one-bedroom apartment.

It worked. He moved to Florida to sponge on his brother.

"I don't care if you ARE still in school," Pat finally had the guts to say. "At 30, you're out of here!"

"Don't set up a room for me," said Zane, just before the family moved into a new home. He had one more semester in college and already had an apartment of his own. Mom and Dad sadly took him at his word, although there was an extra bedroom. But guess who was the first to hang pictures—in that room.

Mary from Edgecomb, Maine prided herself on her cooking. She assumed that was why son Jack enjoyed being home, particularly at mealtime. But Jack moved to Houston and began rooming with a friend. He called to report his enthusiasm.

"Peter's such a wonderful cook!" he bragged. "He cooks all kinds of vegetables, onions, eggs and any kind of restaurant leftovers in the frying pan, and it's so good you don't even have to put ketchup on it."

Eth says the international distress signal is NOT "mayday!" It's "Mama!"

Her daughters, Margery, 34, and Judy, 32, were driving from Pennsylvania to North Carolina with Margery's three preschool children. When the car broke down on the highway, did her Phi Beta Kappa girls call a wrecker in Virginia? No indeed! They called Mama in North Carolina.

Nothing is ever quite the same, after a child has left home and then comes back.

Judy, a "freewheeling" teen of the '70s came in on a college break to find that her room had been disturbed and her stash of grass was missing. She knew she was in for it BIG.

Sure enough, when she went downstairs, there was the stash in the middle of the kitchen table. Mom was seated grimly behind it. "Is this what I think it is?" she asked.

"What do you think it is?"

"You know what I think it is."

After a Titanic iceberg silence, Mom spoke again. "Could you show me how to do this? My bridge club wants to know."

RIDICULOUS ROLE REVERSAL

When does it happen? The mother becomes the child; the child, the parent. Too soon.

Trudging back to the car after a long shopping spree, Betsy realized that she had dropped her car keys somewhere. But where? Panicked, she scooped up Sianna, 2, and hurriedly retraced her steps. During the search, she whined about her own carelessness and how impatient she was to get home. Sianna didn't make a sound.

Finally at the third store, Betsy spotted her key chain on the checkout counter. "I found them!" she shouted.

As she snatched the keys, Sianna took Betsy's face between her two small hands. Looking her straight in the eyes, she said, "I'm proud of you, Mama," and gave her a kiss.

While tossing toys into the toy box, Elizabeth asked her daughter, Grace, 2, for help.

She came over to her mother and said, "But Mommy, you're doing such a good job!" She then patted Elizabeth on the back and returned to her room.

Never have a son who is a stand-up comic. Jeff's mom gave permission for him to tell stories about her. His favorite was:

"My mom's a magician. Every time she walks down the street, she turns into...a bar."

Margery complimented her boss, Lois, on the clothes she was wearing one morning.

"Thanks," she said. "It's my godmother outfit. I have several."

"Is that what you wear to church when the baby is baptized?" asked Margery.

"Oh no. Whenever I wear it, my children say, 'God, Mother. You're not going to wear THAT are you?'"

When asked whether their family had experienced role-reversal yet, one parent didn't have to ponder a moment. "My daughters have been telling me where to go for years."

Once in a while, the older one does the reversal.

When hubby Alex made social plans that did not include Fran, he automatically assumed she would be the children's caregiver during his absence. But when she made plans that did not include him, he insisted that she get a baby sitter. With such a double standard, she felt that she had no spontaneity in her schedule, while he felt free to accept a client's or friends' last-minute invitation. This caused a bit of resentment on her part. Fran picks up the story from here:

Last night, my daughter overheard the two of us "discussing" this situation after she and her brother were put to bed. In the car driving to school the next morning, she wanted to talk about it.

"Mommy, were you and Daddy arguing last night?"

"Well, honey...let's see...not really." (Should I be honest? Evasive? I'm trying to think fast!) "We were just talking...trying to work out a problem."

"Oh?" she asked. "What kind of problem?"

"Well..." I plunge in. "Daddy went to two...sort of parties this weekend without letting Mommy know in advance, and to be truthful, it hurt my feelings that he wasn't spending time with us, the family, over the weekend." (All of Alex's law school cronies are turning 40. There is suddenly a swarm of "surprise" get-togethers among the guys.)

Chrissy listened attentively, staring out the window, but made no response.

So I added, "Daddy doesn't see us much during the week when he's so busy, and I thought he should be spending some time with you and Will—and me—when he's not working. I mean, he's *never* around anymore! Especially since the firm's had to down-size."

Now, I realize it's absurd to use your 8-year-old as a therapist, but I was on a roll. I needed some understanding! "And I just don't think he should run around with all his old buddies having a great time without checking with me—with us—first!" There! It was out.

Chrissy turned, chin tilted upward, eyes half closed. She had one eyebrow raised, exactly as I do when I interrogate her.

105

I smiled feebly.

"Did *you* get any party invitations this weekend, Mommy?" she asked, pointing her finger at me.

"Well, no..." I cleared my throat. "But that's not the point." (Is it?)

"Because, if you're not being a good friend, you *won't* get party invitations. That's what you tell Will and me."

Sometimes children seem to be the mature ones; parents, the juveniles.

Like most kids, Matt just had to have that cereal that had been so heavily-advertised on all the TV kiddie shows. He got his way, and the next day was crunching his first bite from the cherished box. He chewed and chomped, finally swallowing. "This stuff tastes like dog food!" he cried in a most un-Mikey manner.

"It is," said Mom, winking at Dad.

Mother and Father from Georgia told me about their 1901 vintage home, which sounded very much like the Bates homeplace in *Psycho*. They confirmed it with an anecdote about their daughter's boyfriend who came to call and asked, "Y'all sleep here at night?"

Then Mother told of all the farm animals and various other critters who live on their property and in the home. Ah hah! I thought: the Addams family lives on Old MacDonald's farm.

As though reading my mind, Mother told how their children, when hitching a ride from friends' parents, would ask the driver to let them off next door. Then they'd scoot through the woods to get home.

The smoke alarm went off at 5:30 a.m. Awakened by the blasting, everyone in the household rushed outside to safety. No fire. Sleepily returning to bed, Christi, her brother Torey and her sister Cori slid onto rice between the sheets. "April Fool!" chuckled their mom.

Later that day, when Mother went to the store, Christi, 12, and Cori, 18, got revenge. Upon her return, Mom saw "Gotcha!" written in shaving cream across the front lawn. Hanging out the windows and on every tree were all of her bras and panties.

Marilyn's son once observed, "Mom, you're just an arrested adolescent."

"Ah..." she said, "but I have no convictions."

This mom, according to the child, abdicated her role.

Mom, raised by strict elderly grandparents, was determined to allow her own children more choices and more chances to be involved in teenage activities. That was sometimes more freedom than Judy wanted.

One night, a 10th-grade classmate stopped by the house and asked her to ride to the Dairy Queen with him. On a school night. Around 9 p.m.

Judy fell back on the old standby of every teenager who doesn't want to do something. "My mother won't let me," she said, filling her voice with just the right tinge of bitterness.

Hah! Not only did Mom say, "Sure, go ahead," practically waving her out the door, but she added, "Just be home by midnight."

Judy turned her back to her unwanted date, facing Mom, to signal with her eyes and mouth: "Say 'no.' Say 'no.'"

She didn't know whether to laugh or cry when Mom responded with, "That's some nervous tic you're developing, Honey. How many times have I told you—relax and have a little fun?"

Some mamas don't seem to "know their place."

She met her newly-engaged son for lunch at a restaurant one day, groping to adjust to her new role in his life. "I've heard," she said, "that the mother of the groom should wear beige and keep her mouth shut."

"Oh Mom," he said sympathetically, "you don't have to wear beige."

An Italian mother, Mistica enjoyed the attention of her grown son, Leo, who was still living with her. Sometimes he even took her to the movies.

One evening, Sylvia, who was dating Leo, suggested that they swing back by the house to pick up Mistica and treat her to a movie. They went in to tell her the good news.

Mistica was delighted and rushed out to the car.

"Mom," said Leo, "you're supposed to sit in the back seat."

Mistica was not ready for this switch in roles. "I'm no going to be a back driver's seat."

"My husband and I left Roanoke to move closer to his widowed mother in Spartanburg, so that he could take care of her," said Bet. "And what do you think *she* did?"

"What?"

"At age 72, she eloped with an old beau and moved to Columbia."

Occasionally, an outsider reverses a mother's role.

A video producer had been called in to shoot a film for her client, who was promoting an educational organization. The young producer, Terry, was positioning three chairs together to get a good close-up of the educators. A large white-haired woman with a formidable carriage entered the set and immediately repositioned the furniture.

"Wait a minute," said Terry. "I need them the way I had them to get a good shot."

"I've been a principal for 40 years," announced the woman haughtily, "and I'm going to sit *here*."

Well aware of the difference in their age, Terry sucked in her breath. "You may have been a principal for 40 years, but I'm the director and, on a movie set, the director trumps a principal."

After a tense silence, the woman deferred to her director.

Terry looked over at her client, who was watching in awe. After the shoot, the client called Terry aside. "You're the first person who's ever told my mother what to do."

They are all adults, but the eldest doesn't act like one. Or the younger people prefer parent status.

Their children were grown and gone. But they would come back for a meal once in a while. On one such occasion, both daughters and their son were there. Suddenly they all got quite serious.

"Mom, we need to talk," a daughter began. They sat her down and started saying something about having consulted with other people. Together, they had come to the conclusion that they must confront her. Intervene.

She clutched her own hands. What kind of problem do they think I have? she wondered. They went on and on.

"We don't want you to indulge in this any longer," one said.

Then the oldest took charge. "Mom, we've consulted with Chickanon and they agree you're a chickoholic. You must stop serving so much chicken."

Their three adult children announced that, for their anniversary, Robbye and Harold were invited to enjoy a wonderful dinner at the home of one of their daughters.

The threesome began by offering valet service when Mom and Dad drove up. At the front door, one of them was handing out glasses of champagne. Flowers were on the table. Another announced that, in just a moment, they would be served a "wonderful dinner." And then they brought out fish sticks, frozen french fries and green Jell-o gelatin.

Mom recognized the menu immediately. Every Friday night, when a baby sitter would come for the ritual Mom's-and-Dad's-night-out, that is what she would give them.

Despite the "Why does the Jell-o always have to be green?" and "Can't we have something else?" complaints, that's what they got: fish sticks, frozen french fries and green Jell-o, by Robbye's definition, a "wonderful dinner."

On her first visit to her married son's home, Debby made good on a years-earlier promise. She immediately asked, "Where's the coffee table so I can put my feet up on it?" Glass in hand, she placed it on the wood, ignoring the coaster.

At Christmastime, Mom and Stepdad were visiting daughter Bert. Stepdad habitually took an afternoon nap on the sofa, filling the living room with his snores. Expecting guests on Christmas Eve afternoon, Bert saw him heading for the sofa and asked Mom to please encourage her husband to sleep upstairs that day. Mom stomped to his side and shook him. "Get up! We have to go to our room!" she said in a bit of a twit.

He obeyed, and she joined him.

A little later, Bert's husband George arrived and immediately noticed the peaceful lower floor. "Bert," he said with a grin, "did you send those old people to 'time out'?"

"Yep."

Darlene and her sister were trying to help their mother adjust in a retirement home.

"How much is this costing me?" Mom wanted to know.

"Uh, $750 a month," replied Darlene.

"WHAT! How horrible. I'll have to move!" She ranted on about the terrible expense, while both girls tried to explain that it covered all her meals and numerous other services.

That satisfied her for awhile, but the next time they saw her, she asked again, "How much is this costing me?"

Knowing that her mother's memory wasn't what it once was, Darlene quickly replied. "Oh about $250."

"WHAT! How horrible. I'll have to move!"

"Why won't you let me buy a new car?" Hannah whined like a 2-year-old. "You're mean!" she accused as though a teenager balking at her mama's rules.

But Raymond wasn't her mama. He was her only child.

At 91, Hannah had recently had a serious accident, totalling her car. Her version was the opposite of what was on the police report. She claimed she was traveling south and turning right when a man wearing a hat and driving a white sedan screeched his brakes behind her, swerved around—all the way around—and hit her Cadillac on the right front fender (a feat, which Raymond, 59, said defies the laws of physics).

The policeman (who lied, according to Hannah) reported that she was traveling north and turning left when she hit a dark green car driven by a woman with a child in the front seat. The woman wore no hat. But she had head injuries and her child's leg was broken in six places. Hannah says she saw no firetruck or ambulance, only the wrecker that towed her car away.

Although "making an unsafe movement" was attributed to her on the police report, the state that had given her, at age 90, a license for five years with no road test, did not revoke it.

And so night after night, week after week, she berated Raymond to let her buy a new car, accusing him of being an unloving son.

After trying to explain rationally, he resorted to "It's just not safe for you to be driving."

"I'm a better driver than you are!" she would retort. "Besides, I'd rather die in my car than in bed."

"Yes, Mother, but you might take someone with you."

Her reply: "People die in auto accidents every day."

Truth was, Raymond had nothing to do with "letting" her make a purchase. She kept enough money in her checking account to buy the luxury car of her choice. But she was too cheap to pay the cab fare to get to the dealership. That was the only thing that gave him peace.

Then, one Thursday night, she called and asked him to come to her retirement home on Saturday afternoon because she had something important to discuss. He agreed, and they set a time. On Friday, she mentioned that the dealership was having an open house Saturday to show new Cadillacs, and she wanted to go buy one.

Raymond did not sleep Friday night. "Pray for rain," he begged everyone he saw Saturday morning, vainly hoping that a deluge would deter her.

Finally, he came up with a plan. He carefully wrote on the back of his business card: "Under NO circumstances should you sell this woman a car." With a stern stare, he would hand it to the salesman.

At the appointed time, mother and son browsed the showroom. Raymond kept his hand near the pocket with the business card.

Ah, but Hannah was her own worst enemy. She wore the clothes she used to wear for gardening—an old pair of men's pants and a dirty plaid shirt, untucked. Because she had not bought a pair of shoes since her favorite chunky heels came out in the '60s, her pumps were tattered with little curls of leather peeling off. Raymond could almost hear the assorted salespeople wondering if she were a homeless person. Then Hannah wandered over to the refreshment table and answered their unspoken question by stuffing her pocketbook with food.

"Nobody waited on us," she said huffily. "Let's go!"

GRANDMOTHERHOOT

When I was little, I thought any woman with gray hair was a granny. From the other end of the spectrum, I see that grandmothers are quite colorful (as are their children's children). And all grandmas are not cut by the same cookie cutter.

"At my house, we call Reese's Peanut Butter Cups 'green vegetables,'" said well-seasoned grandmother Bet. "Then when my grandchildren go home, they can honestly tell their mama they've had their green vegetables."

Grandmama, who had been baby-sitting with Kim, 4, met Mom and Dad at the door looking quite frazzled. Shaking her head, she blew a stray wisp of hair off her forehead. "I don't know what got into that child, today," she said. "Everything had to be her way—what she wanted to eat, what she wanted to play, even what she wanted to wear."

"You don't say," commented Dad, as he stared out the window. Kim was squatted barefoot in her sandbox digging away happily in the 95-degree July heat—looking like Little Red Riding Hood in her red wool winter coat and matching bonnet.

Now wouldn't you think that a grandmother would want every baby picture available of her grandchild? Not this one.

Cacki had a collection of photos taken two weeks apart and a 30-minute video of her little girl. She offered a print for the grandparents' refrigerator. "No thanks," said Grandmother. "I'll wait 'til she's born."

Another grandmother had a totally different attitude.

She was very proud of her new grandbaby.

So proud that she displayed the ultrasound photo where all her friends and relatives could see it: at her daughter's (the baby's mother's) wedding. So? So it's the '90s!

113

Expecting a visit from her 2-year-old granddaughter, Sianna, Ruth was frustrated when her dishwasher broke. She quickly dialed the number for her repairman and got his father.

"My son's on vacation," he said, "But I can come."

Later, Ruth heard a car come up the driveway. She called out the window in a high-pitched voice. "Yoohoo! Hi sweetie! How's my honey pie," she sang. "Get in here so I can give you a big hug and kiss!"

She threw open the door to see the repairman.

"Exactly how well do you know my son?" he asked.

The day Doris discovered that her 46-year-old daughter was finally having a baby—triplets in fact—she danced around the house with lighted sparklers.

Burned a hole in her fine living room carpet.

Granny and Granddad had taken 3-year-old Bonny to church with them and were headed to a restaurant for lunch. Bonny had just used the little traveling potty they kept in the car. Granny rolled down the window and threw out the contents. Well, out momentarily. Air currents sprinkled and splashed pee all over her Sunday dress and "Saturday hairdo."

Said Dee, an attractive entrepreneur with a 27-year-old son: "To my knowledge, I'm nobody's grandmother."

Like mothers, they can be surprised by what their grand-kids do.

Grandmother was at the hospital talking with the Baptist preacher. Her grandson Jackie kept grabbing her around the legs, yanking at her shorts. The elastic waistband stretched, causing the pants to fall and redness to rise like mercury from Grandmother's toes to her head.

Grandma Gertie was honored when her grandson with a brand new driver's license offered to take her out to lunch. She was still beaming when they wheeled into the drive-thru line of McDonald's.

Grandma and Granddad were baby-sitting with Buddy, while their daughter was at work. Granddad was supposed to be cleaning out the vacuum cleaner and setting it up to clean another room. Somehow he got sidetracked by a football game on TV in the playroom.

That's when Grandma heard the sound of a brook. Unnoticed, Buddy had put the vacuum cleaner hose into the washing machine, sucking out all the water. By the time they could stop him, the laundry room *and* the playroom floors were a soapy lake.

That marked the first day Buddy was ever sent to his room!

Bet's strapping teenage grandson was leaning against the car, twanging the antenna, as she reached into the trunk for a bag of groceries. Having second thoughts, she sarcastically said, "Wait a minute, Douglas. *You* take the groceries in the house for *me*, and *I'll* twiddle the aerial for *you*."

Douglas grinned and promptly gathered up the groceries, and Bet took his place twiddling the antenna. As he headed for the door, he turned around, studied her briefly and remarked archly, "You're not doing it right, Grandmother."

But have you heard? Grandkids say the *cutest* things.

Her four-year-old grandson was bringing her a storybook. But Madeleine realized that she didn't have her glasses. "I'm sorry, I can't read it," she gently told him.

That's okay, Grandma," he said sympathetically. "I can't read either."

Grandmother Grace was having a hard time getting her little grandson, Gregg, to come inside. She called him until irritation changed her tone of voice and raised the volume.

Gregg came a'running with a look of disapproval. "Grandmother, you haven't had your nap yet!"

While Bobbie's 8-year-old granddaughter was visiting her for a week, the child's 13-year-old brother Justin wrote a note, which said in part, "Grandmom: You can have Kate anytime ...and keep her as long as you want."

Grandma Phyllis was changing to go to the pool. She didn't have the curtain pulled all the way closed, and little Sarah, 4, peeked in. "Gramps! Don't look!" she cried. "It's not a pretty sight."

Anna's mother called the child's grandmother. "Linda, would you please say 'hello' to Anna? She's been walking around the house calling 'MawMaw, MawMaw.'"

Pleased, Linda waited for Anna to take the receiver. "Hey, Darlin'!"

"Hey, PawPaw!"

Katy was sitting on Grandmother Bert's lap scratching her leg. "Gramma, why did God make mosquitos?"

"I don't know Katy."

The 4-year-old thought a minute. "Well, when I go to Heaven, I'm going to tell Him to stop. We have enough."

While her daughter and son-in-law were repairing old plaster walls in a spare room, Genevieve went over to baby-sit with the grandchildren.

Soon, Mark, 3, was gazing up at her from her lap. "Mom-Mom, my dad has real good stuff for patching up cracks," he said. "If you want, you can have some to fix up all these cracks in your neck."

Bobbie told of Kate's startling question: "Grandmother, are you too old to take me next door to play with Eric?"

She put on a look of determination. "I would've *crawled* to take her to Eric's!"

Sometimes what they say is not so cute.

Family and friends of an elderly man filed into the church for his funeral. His wife was seated in the honored place at the front with her grandson at her side.

During a silent moment at this most solemn occasion, the little boy put his hands on his hips and squawked, "You see, Granny, I *told* you not to be so mean to him!"

The 5-year-old had been discussing her great-grandmother's impending visit.

"I used to have another great-grandmother," Emily reminded her paternal grandmother. "But she's deadmeat."

"What?"

"You know. Sometimes, Mama says 'If you do that one more time, you're deadmeat!'"

Bert was outdone with 3-year-old Katy that day. "What does Gramma say when you whine?"

Katy didn't pause a moment. "Dammit."

Same grandmother, trying to be subtle: "Katy, what do you think chocolate milk would look like on Gramma's white carpet?"

Katy: "Horse poop."

So much for subtle.

During a visit, Grandma Janie was sewing while her granddaughter was playing nearby.

"How long are you going to stay?" asked Rebecca. Before Janie could answer, Rebecca explained why she wanted to know. "I love you, but I'm tired of you."

Sue raced to her husband's home office to retrieve the FAX coming in. "Ben pooped," it said in her 5-year-old grandson's scrawl.

And what did she do with this startling news? Folded it into an envelope and mailed it to Ben's great-grandmother with a note: "See what grandmotherhood's like now?"

More startling news about grandmothers of the '90s:

Contrary to popular belief, grandmothers *do* think about sex. A Florida grandmom bought a Fredericks-of-Hollywood-style nightie of sexy black lace to entice her husband.

He came to bed and stared. Finally, he spoke. "Who died?"

Another grandma's perspective:

Joanne was showing me photos of her 17-month-old grand-quads—three boys and a girl.

"How adorable!" I cooed. "Bet you love to visit them. How long do you stay?"

Her skin crinkled as she smiled. "Not very long."

On being Grammy:

Joy dropped our grandson Chas, 2, by at 8 a.m. so I could baby-sit.

After he trashed "his" room, I read several books to him and blew bubbles to his delight. He tried on Grandy's shoes and my hand cream. Then we played with each of his toys inside and out. We took a long walk, threw rocks in the creek, washed his hands and other moving parts, ate a snack and played peek-a-boo. Exhausted, I looked at my watch. It was 9 a.m.

Will my hair turn gray? Not as long as I can crawl to the beauty salon.

About three years ago, I told my friend Ethel that I would soon become a grandmother.

"You'll love it," she said. "And then you'll know why they call it 'grand.'"

That's true. Most of the time.

MotherHoot
TIPS FOR SANITY

From pregnancy through grandmotherhood...
* Always have damp baby wipes—for yourself.

During pregnancy...
* Be absolutely certain you know "how it happened."
* Check to be sure your shoes match *before* you stand up.
* Never put your specimen in a whiskey bottle.
* Don't hug mere acquaintances after your water breaks.
* Avoid swimming with crocodiles during mating season.
* Forgive your husband, no matter what he says or does; you may need him later.

While trying to think of a name...
* Never name a child while under anesthesia; she shouldn't have to go through life with a handle like Femally or Placenta.
* Avoid product names. Charmin' could end up "T.P."
* Be certain you know the meaning of a foreign word like "Latrine" or the Armenian word for nausea.
* Be aware of the initials a child will carry with him forever. For instance, if your last name begins with "S," don't call him Anthony Stephen.
* Likewise, imagine whom a daughter might marry. Picha (pronounced "picka") might end up with Mr. Bugger.
* Commemorating an event is not such a great idea. Little girls don't like to be called "Hurricane" as in Hurricane Alicia or "Remember" as in Remember September.
* When naming a child for a famous person, avoid using the title as a first name, like Queen Elizabeth Brown and General Stonewall Jackson.
* Be sure to name your child on time, lest his legal name end up Baby Boy Moffatt.

When your children are babies...
* Remember: the teddy bears go on the front.
* Keep in mind that very few people hiccup for 30 years and a stuffy nose is not life-threatening.
* Don't fret if it's 6 p.m. and you haven't dressed yet.

* It is important to get the holes in the nipple just the right size for the *first* baby.
* When in public, burp the baby, not yourself.

While they are in the "terrible twos"...

* Have a nervous breakdown before the birthday and stay in a sanatorium for a year—or plan to retire there when the stage has passed.
* Remember: no crib sides, kiddie gate, dead bolt, live wire or chloroform will keep him in.
* Most tips from other parents will not apply, because your child will act his age in an entirely unique way.
* Keep your kid on a leash and let the dog run free.
* Wait until he is 3 before you take him out in public.
* Don't be surprised if your extended family stops visiting and your friends invite you to "adults only" parties.
* In the "year of the potty," be careful of whom you ask if they want to "come inside and pee."
* Never take a child in training pants into a store with a toilet display.
* Don't introduce Winnie-the-Pooh to your kid as "Pooh."
* Train them before you leave them on their own (daddies, that is).

If you have twins, triplets or quads...
* Order strait jackets, one for each of you.

When they say something outrageous...

* Never try to guess which "F word" he wants permission to use.
* If your youngster challenges you to dance naked in high heels, do it for Daddy.
* Don't let your feelings get hurt when your son tells others that he loves them (others like trees, cars, whatever).
* Despite his allergies, don't allow your daughter talk you into getting a cat and letting Papa move out.
* It's okay to impersonate God, when your child assumes "you" can't see her.
* Agree with your child if he thinks PMS spells "be quiet."
* You do not have to answer questions such as "What would you do if a robber threw up on your shoes?" or "What kind of underwear does God wear?" or even "Why do I have to sleep alone, when you can sleep with Daddy?"

* Pretend you don't know your child when he or she says (to a pregnant woman) "I know what YOU'VE been doing," (to an NFL cheerleader) "I'm going to be a doctor; my mommy says cheerleaders are clueless," (or to the minister) "Would you please spit into this cup. Mama says you're full of holy spit, and I want to see how full of holes your spit really is."

When they do something outrageous...
* Blame yourself if you referred to your diaphragm as a "little cup" and then found out that your kids drank out of it.
* Blame Dad if your sons served homemade wine to friends in their new neighborhood while you were out grocery shopping.
* If you were a kid once, you don't have to ask what they are doing when you hear belt buckles rattling behind a locked door.
* Scratch a baby sitter's name off your list, if your son pees on her head so you won't leave him.
* Ask the kindergarten teacher what her class has been learning if your daughter's snowman is anatomically correct.
* Try to sound appreciative when you thank your son for waxing the clean kitchen floor with bacon grease or your daughter for baking you a cake made of eggs, chocolate pudding mix and French dressing.
* Question your teenager's IQ when he spray-paints your gray car, vinyl top and all, a tacky gold so you won't recognize his new vehicle (which still has your license plate attached).

When they are trying to figure out what birds and bees do...
* Admit to your two children that, yes, you and Dad did that *twice*.
* With a video camera running, if your child points out your wedding picture to a stranger and says, "That's my mommy; I'm in her tummy," you must speak right in the microphone to assert, "He was born years later. I have the papers to prove it."
* However, while watching a bride and groom kiss at their wedding, just smile and put a finger to your lips if your child asks, "Has he sprinkled the pollen on her yet?"
* If, as a grandmother, you try to assume the straightforwardness of the '90s, you can claim you don't remember when your grandson wants to know if you "do it with your clothes off."
* You need not correct your son when he states that the seventh commandment says "Don't cut adult trees."
* And never, never correct your daughter when she pencils in a space marked "sex" with "haven't had it yet."

When those teen years are too trying for words...
* Bear in mind that you may have to wait for an apology until your child has teenagers.
* Remind them that they are *lucky* if they get caught.
* When your renegade runs away, call a family conference to decide whether you want to take her back.
* Remember that, although they will beg you to go to their games, you are not allowed to wave.
* When a police officer calls at midnight to say that your son is in jail, try telling him to inform your son that "It's entirely too late for him to be out, and he must come home immediately!"
* If your son's pet snake or tarantula gets lost in the house, leave the premises until it has been found, even if that takes a month.
* When you find the remains of a block of ice after you were away from home overnight, do not believe the line about some "freak hailstorm" the night before.
* It's okay to agree with AOL chat room moms who type in caps (which is shouting):"THERE'S NOTHING FUNNY ABOUT BEING THE MOTHER OF A TEENAGER."

When they try to fill your empty nest again...
* Brace for it: they WILL return—with roommates, pets, "significant other," spouse and/or children.
* Find out if his friends have a spare room in their apartment and offer to pay half the rent.
* Sell your four-bedroom house to buy a one-bedroom apartment. (Then he will go sponge on his brother instead.)
* Announce, "I don't care if you ARE still in school—at 30, you're out of here!"

If they try to pull a ridiculous role reversal on you...
* Pull one on your own: on a visit to your married child's home, put your feet on the coffee table and place your glass on the wood, ignoring the coaster.

As a grandmother...
* Never assume you're not a granny if the kids are over 18.
* If you get so fussy that your grandkid asks if you've had your nap yet, take one.
* When you ask a grandkid, "What does Gramma say when you whine?" you shouldn't be surprised if she says, "Dammit."
* Always have Reese's Peanut Butter Cups—instead of green vegetables.

Give your favorite expectant mom, mother, grandmother or mother-in-law some chuckles to brighten her day! Order personalized gift copies now!

_____copies *MotherHoot, the Lighter Side of Motherhood*
True tales from pregnancy through grandmotherhood.
1999. 325 tales. 128 pp. ISBN:0-9640606-8-X
Cartoons by Loyd Dillon   Paperback @ $9.95 $_____

Or try Margaret Bigger's wedding humor books:

_____copies *You've GOT to Have a Sense of Humor To Have a Wedding*
Humorous, outrageous & disastrous tales. Advice, too!
1997. 587 tales. 128 pp. ISBN:0-9640606-5-5
Cartoons by Loyd Dillon
3rd printing, April 1998   Paperback @ $9.95 $_____
_____copies *There's No Such Thing as a Perfect Wedding* (Down Home Press)
True wedding tales, odd, funny and disastrous.
1991. 209 tales. 96 pp. ISBN: 1-878086-04-9
Cartoons by Tim Rickard
9th printing, April 1998   Paperback @ $7.95 $_____

Autographed?_____If you want them personalized, please list names on the other side of form and state whether they are the bride & groom, mother of the bride (she usually needs humor the most), mother of the groom, minister, rabbi, priest, florist, wedding director, photographer, etc. If it is the mother of the bride (MOB) /groom (MOG), please give the first names of the couple.

Other books of true-experience anecdotes by ABB:

_____copies *Gray-Haired Grins & Giggles*
Guess what - Grandy & Grammy have a sense of humor, too!
1995. 160 tales. 128 pp. ISBN:0-9640606-3-9
True tales from 45 authors. Cartoons by Loyd Dillon.
4th printing, June 1996.   Paperback @ $12.95 $_____
With the seal of approval of N.A.V.H.:
Large print edition. 1998   Paperback @ $13.95 $_____
_____copies *World War II: It Changed Us Forever*
From the battlefront to the homefront and places in between.
1994. 93 tales. 140 pp. ISBN:0-9640606-0-4
33 authors tell it like it was! Vintage photos.
2nd printing, July 1994. Paperback @ $12.95 $_____

MORE ON NEXT PAGE

Bigger's guide to recording memoirs:

_____copies *Recalling Your Memories on Paper, Tape or Videotape*
Self-help guide to preserving memoirs & photos.
Also how to help parents record memories.
1996. 160 pp. ISBN:0-9640606-4-7
Excerpts from seniors' family booklets.
Vintage photos.   Paperback @ $13.95 $_____

And a regional book of one-liners:

_____copies *You Can Tell You're a Charlottean If...*
244 ways that people from Charlotte, NC differ from the
rest of the world. Margaret Bigger & Betsy Webb
1998. 96 pp. ISBN:0-9640606-6-3
Cartoons by Loyd Dillon.
Head Scratchers & Queenz Quiz.   Paperback @ $7.95 $_____

Shipping & handling $2 up to 5 books; $4 up to 10 $_____

NC residents add 6% tax $_____

TOTAL $_____

Please mail check or money order with this form to:

A. Borough Books
P.O. Box 15391
Charlotte, NC 28211

Name_____

Address_____

City, State, Zip_____

Phone #_____

Specify here how you want your books to be personalized.

Contributor's Form

Your personal anecdotes for Volume 2 of **MotherHoot**

Check chapter title:
____Expectant, Expectorant Behavior
____Who? Why?
____New Mom, New Babe, No Instructions
____Terrible Twos - Terrible for Mom
____Said *WHAT?*
____Did *WHAT?*
____Crime & Punishment, Kid Style
____Birds & Bees & Adult Trees
____Somebody Control This Child!
____Teens - Too Trying for Words
____Mother Embarrasses Herself, No Help from the Kids
____You Can't Outlaw Mothers-in-Law
____There's No Such Thing as an Empty Nest
____Ridiculous Role Reversal
____GrandmotherHoot
____New chapter: _____

Your favorite motherhood anecdote:

More anecdotes (specify chapter titles):

Note: We will use only first names in the book, but we will notify you by postcard if your story makes the publisher's cut.

Name _____

Address _____

City, State, Zip _____

Phone # _____

Please mail this form to:

A. Borough Books
P.O. Box 15391
Charlotte, NC 28211